cl⊙se -ups

Close-Ups is a series of pocket guides to the world of film from *Little White Lies* and William Collins. In the title you are holding, our hope is that you find a fresh, personal exploration of a particular director, actor, movement or genre. We hope that you will join our authors in their efforts to look at movies through a new lens.

David Jenkins
Editor
Little White Lies Magazine

close -ups

NEW YORK MOVIES

MARK ASCH

WILLIAM
COLLINS

Thrive, cities—bring your freight,
bring your shows, ample and
sufficient rivers,

Expand, being than which none
else is perhaps more spiritual,

Keep your places, objects than
which none else is more lasting.

- *Walt Whitman,*
"Crossing Brooklyn Ferry"

CONTENTS

INTRODUCTION

The Warriors (Walter Hill, 1979)

I n *The Warriors*, a teenage gang fight their way from one end of the subway to the other. They return to their home turf of Coney Island after an all-night odyssey shot in Riverside Park and Evergreen Cemetery, on the streets of Hell's Kitchen and Long Island City, the elevated tracks in Borough Park and Cypress Hills and the underground stations at Hoyt-Schermerhorn and Union Square, and in innumerable gray subway cars covered in scrabbled Sharpie graffiti tags. Each gang has their own tribal uniform: the Baseball Furies in their fright makeup and bats; the Punks in their rollerskates and overalls; the Gramercy Riffs in their orange martial arts robes.

The Warriors is accurate in its broad contours about the necessity of improvised itineraries when dealing with New York's late-night train service, as well as in its depiction of a city that can feel intimidatingly territorial. Each gang is its own subculture, with its own aesthetic, hierarchy and history, and woe betide anyone who disrespects their priority. It's their home—you're just visiting.

The city, E. B. White wrote, "carries on its lapel the unexpungeable odor of the long past, so that no matter where you sit in New York you feel the vibrations of great times and tall deeds, of queer people and events and undertakings." So too with the city's cinema. When the Warriors finally make it back to Stillwell Avenue, they walk under overcast off-season skies past shuttered amusements and stilled rides, including the same Cyclone roller coaster where Diana Ross's Dorothy had found her Tin Man in *The Wiz* the year before.

In this book, I follow the New York street grid (though without the leatherette Warriors vest). It's a guidebook, mapping out the scenes, communities, artists and powers-that-be that have staked their claim to this block or that neighborhood, in this moment in time or that one. Chapters are organized chronologically, though some double-feature pairings that communicate from different eras. I've restricted my selections here to films shot significantly on location (with the caveat that "significant" is a flexible word), and to one film per director, in a nevertheless failed attempt to cast a net as wide as the city. I've stuck to fiction features, rather than compete with the direct views of documentaries.

I'm indebted in the writing of this book to my editor, David Jenkins; to the Hekemian family for a place to write and my parents for the lifelong conviction that I had something to say; and to all the past and present citizens of my New York, the film critics, programmers and cinephiles whose advocacy and insight has enriched me as an editor, reader and audience member. My life in New York, at the movies, as a writer, and in so many other ways, would be unimaginable to me without Larissa Kyzer, to whom this book is dedicated.

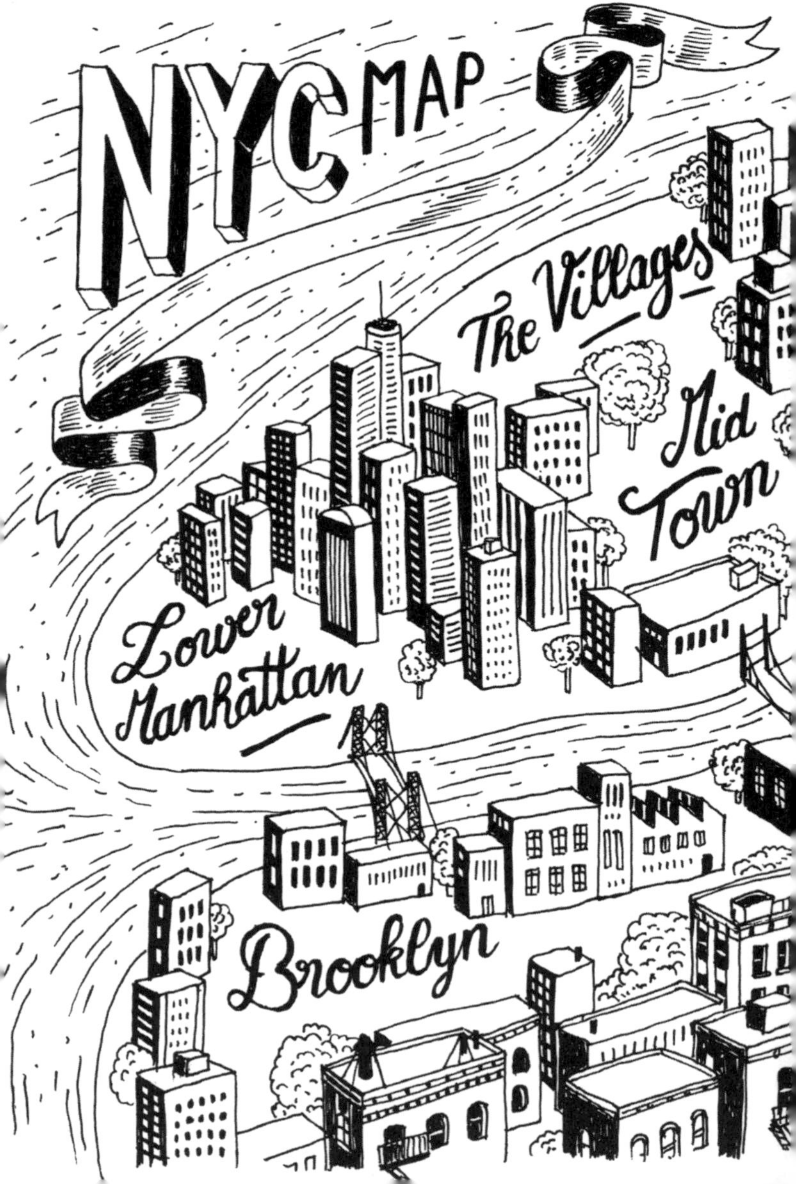
NYC MAP
The Villages
Mid Town
Lower Manhattan
Brooklyn

CENTRAL
PARK

The Window (Ted Tetzlaff, 1949) / *Home Alone 2: Lost in New York* (Chris Columbus, 1992)

A window peeper knows his neighbor has committed a murder, but no one else believes him—except the killer. When Alfred Hitchcock filmed Cornell Woolrich's pulp story "It Had to Be Murder" as *Rear Window* (1954), he built his Greenwich Village panopticon on a massive Paramount set with a dozen fully furnished apartments, all of city life opened up in a dollhouse-like cross-section promising savvy familiarity with the lives of others, and whiff of stranger danger. But "The Boy Cried Murder," another Woolrich story with the same premise, had already been filmed as *The Window*—on location, in the East 100s.

Sleeping on his fire escape on a sweltering summer night, young Tommy Woodry sees the couple upstairs murder a man, but gets lectured about telling tales by his proud parents. Director Ted Tetzlaff, Hitchcock's Director of Photography on *Notorious* (1946), sets the noirish scene with the rumbling tracks and chiaroscuro shadows cast by the Third Avenue elevated train, and shoots the surrounding cross streets through fire escapes and jungle canopies

of backyard clotheslines. With Mom visiting her sick sister and Pop on the night shift, Tommy is as trapped as *Rear Window*'s wheelchair-bound Jimmy Stewart when the neighbors call.

Bobby Driscoll, who plays Tommy, starred in Disney's live-action Boomer-baby swashbuckler *Treasure Island* (1950), but fell out of favor with the Mouse House when puberty hit; he got into drugs,

and had been in and out of prison before his body was found in 1968 by two children playing in an abandoned tenement on East 10th Street. Around the time Driscoll's body was buried in an unmarked grave on Hart Island, photographer Bruce Davidson was taking pictures of *The Window*'s old neighborhood, by then known as Spanish Harlem. In his collection *East 100th Street*, kids Tommy's age and younger pose on a stained mattress in the middle of an alley piled high with rubbish and rubble, or in dark rooms with linoleum curling over rotting floorboards, ceilings cracked or swelling. It's a complementary view to the film, which captures an East Side where kids play stickball on the street, or race across sticky-tar rooftops with the towers of midtown remote in the distance. Within years, postwar suburbanization—"white flight" hastened by the integration of neighborhoods—and the wasting-away of the urban tax base would see the decline of *The Window*'s working-class neighborhood into the kind of modern-day ghetto made legendary by representations less sensitive than Davidson's.

Out the other side of this chapter in New York history, another too-precocious child star stops a criminal plot. Through *Home Alone 2: Lost in New York*'s Kevin McCallister (Macaulay Culkin), potential tourists get an eyeful of the Big Apple's landmarks – and a jolt of the fear that may have kept them away. In a template-perfect welcome-to-New York montage, Kevin sticks his head out the window of a Checker Cab to take in the skyline on the way over the Queensboro Bridge; he gazes wide-eyed at Radio City Music Hall, the Statue of Liberty, the World Trade Center ... But when he's outside of his hotel after dark, on West 95th Street and Central Park West, winos yell at him and streetwalkers proposition him. We see the "broken windows" that would be the focus of soon-to-be Mayor Rudy Giuliani and Police Commissioner William Bratton's quality-of-life policing strategy, which cleaned up the visible street-level signifiers of vice in time for the corporate investment then returning to the American urban core. And we see what, precisely, would be meant by "quality of life," as Kevin flashes plastic at Duncan's Toy Chest, standing in for toy superstore F.A.O. Schwarz, and at the Plaza Hotel, the gilded palace at the southeastern corner of the Park.

Kevin, who tips the white-glove service staff in sticks of gum, is a smartass Eloise, the six-year-old Plaza-dweller and cute, prodigious mess-maker of Kay Thompson and Hilary Knight's 1950s picture books. Impulsively indulging in a child's fantasy of luxury, gorging himself on room service junk food and unlimited TV time, Kevin may also remind contemporary viewers of the man who owned the Plaza in 1992. Donald Trump cameos here (he insisted as a condition of the Plaza shoot), directing Kevin to the lobby and then backing away from the camera so his face remains centered in the frame. We see the dual self-promotional strategies of pushy media availability and splashy overleveraged real estate deals that made Trump an avatar of NYC's return to prosperity, shortly before he signed over the Plaza to his debtors to wriggle out of bankruptcy.

Trump's own Broken Windows fantasy of urban property values restored by legal vigilantism was less subtle than Giuliani and Bratton's. In 1989, when a young white woman with an investment-banking job was brutally beaten and raped while jogging in Central Park, five black and Latino teenagers from Harlem were browbeaten into false confessions; Trump took out full-page newspaper ads blaring "Bring Back The Death Penalty. Bring Back Our Police!" When Kevin McCallister first wanders into Central Park, he's terrified of the pigeon dung-caked homeless woman he sees there—but he evolves beyond his initial disgust and terror, and the bird lady helps him to defend the bounty of Duncan's Toy Chest against the thieves played by Joe Pesci and Daniel Stern. (To get the cops' attention, Kevin breaks a window, though he pays for the damage.) Kevin lures Pesci and Stern to the (Hollywood backlot) townhouse his aunt and uncle are gut-renovating in anticipation of rising Upper West Side real-estate prices. The sadism he metes out there—electrocuting them, setting them on fire—would satisfy Bernard Goetz, who opened fire on four black teenage would-be muggers on a 2 train in 1984; or Curtis Sliwa, whose satin-jacketed "Guardian Angels" patrolled subway cars looking for lowlives to rough up throughout the late 70s and 80s; or indeed Travis Bickle, more on whom anon.

Rosemary's Baby (Roman Polanski, 1968) / *Single White Female* (Barbet Schroeder, 1992)

Seen from a dizzying downward angle in the opening credits of *Rosemary's Baby*, the Dakota, on West 72nd Street and Central Park West, resembles a Gothic gingerbread house. Its steep pitched roof, crazy-quilted with turrets and chimneys and dormer windows, seems to hold a storied, shadowy history. The Dakota is the building where John Lennon was shot (and where Yoko Ono still lives); before Rosemary and Guy Woodhouse (Mia Farrow and John Cassavetes) move in, they're warned that the "Bramford," as it's called in the film, has "a rather unsavory reputation" as the former home of cannibals and Satanists.

The Bramford interiors are soundstage sets, but modeled by production designer Richard Sylbert after his friend Lauren Bacall's Dakota apartment. He emphasises contrast between the Woodhouses' apartment, redecorated with yellow wallpaper (!) and airy 60s touches, and the Castevets' next door, with its stuffy furniture and pools of dark wood where the lamplight doesn't reach. Much of the film's tension reverberates out from the relationship between these neighbors, as a young couple try to maintain a properly friendly distance from the old couple having them over for over-familiar dinners, barging in to feed them, recommending doctors. The building itself feeds the tension: Rosemary hears witchy sounds at the Castevets' through the thin walls put up to subdivide the mansion flats of the city's first luxury apartment house; the conjoining door, hidden at the back of a closet, is an unlikely touch, but an accurate one.

As the film's Catholic undertaste seeps through via recent New York history, like Pope Paul VI's visit to Yankee Stadium, so does its metaphorical treatment of pre-natal anxiety overlap with modern urban living. Rosemary's isolation, by the coven who arrange her demonic impregnation and then force-feed her malicious medical advice, is an extreme version of the naturally diverging social orbits of childless couples and their nesting friends. For much of the film, the actor husband who sells Rosemary out to further his career appears simply preoccupied by his uncertain position in a creative field. (Cassavetes overpowers Farrow with constant masculine actorly flourishes, a cavalcade of twitching hands and gritting teeth familiar from his own independent films, funded with gigs like this one.) It's a fairly major historical irony that Roman Polanski directed this hyperspecific account of a young woman's drugging and rape, and society's denial and thus inflammation of her trauma; Rosemary's gaslighting is also a suggestive preview of the manipulations that marked the breakdown of Farrow's partnership with Woody Allen.

"What Roman Polanski did for the Dakota in *Rosemary's Baby*," Vincent Canby wrote in his *New York Times* review of *Single White Female*, "[Barbet] Schroeder attempts to do for the Ansonia, the old great Beaux-Arts pile at the corner of Broadway and 73rd Street." The building looms above the camera in the film's opening minutes, likewise looking like the stuff of legend. (Babe Ruth and Florenz Ziegfeld called the Ansonia home in its residential-hotel days; in the 60s and 70s, as the roof leaked and pipes rusted, its once-grand basement pool was home first to the Continental Baths, whose towel-clad clientele cruised for sex and watched Bette Midler and Barry Manilow perform their first concerts, and then the swingers club Plato's Retreat. The Ansonia eventually went condo.) Here too, a continental director drolly exploits primal feminine Code Red scenarios angled around the intimacy and alienation of New York apartment living, though *Single White Female*'s neighbors eavesdrop through air vents instead of thin walls.

The "Victoria" is accessible to *Single White Female*'s protagonists because of New York's byzantine rent-control laws, rather than the Bramford's presumptive decline and disrepair. With its title referencing classified ads, the film is, in essence, about roommate drama—whether or not somebody's name is on the lease is a pivotal plot point. After Allie (Bridget Fonda) interviews Hedy (Jennifer Jason Leigh) for her spare bedroom, their personality crisis is triggered by passive-aggressive simmering disputes over housekeeping, having boys over, navigating nudity in a shared living space, and borrowing clothes without asking. In *Rosemary's Baby*, Polanski often shot scenes from the next room, the action partially blocked by doorways; Schroeder's camera is often below eye level, like the camera operator is sitting on a box spring on the floor, to emphasize the openness of common areas. Rosemary was trapped in a maze; Allie has no privacy.

While Rosemary got her modish crop from Vidal Sassoon, *Single White Female*'s mid-movie pixie cut comes courtesy SoHo salon John Dellaria—its high-end post-punk edge matches Allie's chic "so New York" wardrobe of dark-hued day-to-night dresses, which Hedy compliments with deceptive self-deprecation. When Hedy mimics Allie's haircut, Schroeder gives her entrance a dizzying trace of *Vertigo*, the greatest of all extreme-makeover movies. (Earlier in the film, the late movie on TV is Jimmy Stewart and Kim Novak atop

the Flatiron Building in *Bell, Book and Candle*—their other semi-supernatural romantic masquerade of 1958, *Vertigo*'s New York "double.") Echoing *Vertigo*'s vortices, Schroeder points his camera down the well of the Ansonia's 17-story open staircase in marble, mahogany and lacy ironwork.

Single White Female doesn't just play with female identity in Hedy's takeover of Allie's personal life—her professional life is hardly less fraught with insecurity and competition. Fashion-software entrepreneur Allie works hard at her work-life balance, and endures sexual harassment to ingratiate herself in a male-dominated field. She is in New York to "establish herself."

Symbiopsychotaxiplasm: Take One (William Greaves, 1968)

A man and woman are having a screaming fight in Central Park —"Don't touch me!" "What's the matter with you?"—when the man is replaced by a new actor, the woman by a new actress, the frame now in split-screen. The fight continues—he's a "faggot," she's "had abortion after abortion"—with a new set of actors, in a different location, before we cut to the film crew, pausing to fix the sound equipment. The whine of feedback becomes

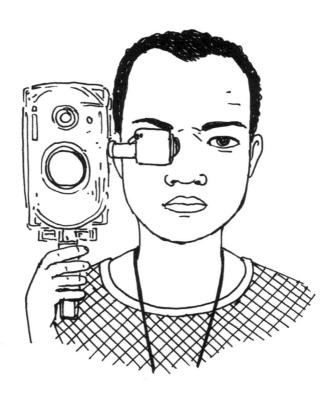

an element in the fusion-jazz score that plays under the opening credits, as we see dog walkers, sunbathers, soccer players. Couples hold hands, picnic and dry hump on the lawns, along the footpaths and under archways. The camera ogles a young woman's ass in blue jeans. The spectacle that opens *Symbiopsychotaxiplasm* is just one private life-as-public performance enacted before a gaze that's voyeuristic, sometimes horned-up, but fundamentally egalitarian: strangers, of all races and body types, sharing the same space on a summer's day. Nor is people-watching a one-way exchange—a flock of kids surround the crew and mug for the camera; a mounted policeman checks permits.

The film is "a feature-length, uh, we-don't-know," writer-director-producer-editor William Greaves explains to the curious cop—a free-for-all of looking and being seen in Central Park, the island of landscaped wilderness shaped into the middle of Manhattan so the upper classes could promenade and the lower classes could spend some time in the sun. The entire street grid funnels into the Park; it's the city's great commons, and the backdrop for enough movies to fill this book and a sequel or two.

An Actors Studio graduate who became a maker of publicly funded documentaries because of the lack of opportunities for black actors, Greaves planned a series of five *Symbiopsychotaxiplasm* films, but *Take One* achieved cult-canonization only gradually, before 2005's *Take 2 ½* at last combined original 16mm footage with new digital footage taken in the Park on the day of the New York Marathon. On one layer of reality, the film is an acting exercise, with multiple pairs of performers cycling through the scene and trying to find their truth (one couple sings their lines). One camera, nominally, films the scene; a second camera films the scene and the first camera crew; and a final camera films the whole gestalt. In practice, the filmmakers bicker over technical issues, and the actors (Don Fellows and Patricia Ree Gilbert for the main part of the film) complain about the script and shit-talk each other into the microphones that are recording at all times. Actors and camera crews cross each other's sightlines, spinning a web of perspectives; the editing is deliberately cacophonous, as sound and image lose track of each other.

"Don't take me seriously," Greaves admonishes his crew, and in rap sessions filmed without him, they question the bad script, his erratic behavior, and the opaque premise of the film (and implicitly encourage our distaste for pervasive on-set sexism and homophobia). Then again, at one point, production manager Bob Rosen looks into the camera and reminds his fellow crew members that, for all they—or any of us in the audience—know, he could be reading from a script right now. Greaves finally reveals to his crew that he was hoping to inspire a "palace revolt," something "not dissimilar to the revolution that's taking place in America today"—or, for that matter, to the antiwar rally and "be-in" that had drawn tens of thousands to Central Park earlier that spring. Decentralising and challenging power and laying bare process, *Symbiopsychotaxiplasm* is radical theater befitting the city's biggest stage.

Manhattan (Woody Allen, 1979) / *Metropolitan* (Whit Stillman, 1990)

"'He adored New York City. He idolized it all out of proportion.' Uh, no. Make that, 'He romanticized it all out of proportion.'" You can tell right from the opening sequence that *Manhattan* is Woody Allen's most ambitious film—when else has he ever edited the first draft of his dialogue? Too, that opening, scored with Gershwin's "Rhapsody in Blue," takes a Best of New York tour—Shakespeare in the Park and the marquees of Broadway, the fountains at Lincoln Center and the Guggenheim's spiral-staircase gallery —that continues throughout the film, shot in silvery black and white by Gordon Willis. Characters leave their Upper East Side garden apartments for smoky conversations at restaurant-cum-boldface-name salon Elaine's, and there's always a classic from the New Yorker Films library playing at Cinema Studio. Woody's Manhattan is the shining city imagined by his youthful surrogate in the Rockaways-set *Radio Days* (1987).

Back in *Manhattan*, Woody's TV writer and novelist Isaac meets Diane Keaton's freelancer-fatale, who makes a seemingly decent living from critiques in the "little magazines." (Today she'd be supplementing online freelance rates with SAT tutoring, and living with roommates in Crown Heights.) When she dismisses Woody's canon as so much Great White Male pomposity, the film anticipates *Manhattan*'s status as a conversation piece in the *New York Review of Books*, where Joan Didion clapped back at its "hermetic self-regard" and references which "reflect exactly the false and desperate knowingness of the smartest kid in the class." Yet Woody and Annie warm to one another on a walk-and-talk that takes them to the foot of the

Queensboro Bridge, lit up and flung out across the predawn sky like a sighing spine.

Characters talk through ambivalent feelings for friends and lovers, and crack wise over their existential despair. ("I finally had an orgasm and my doctor told me it was the wrong kind.") It's urban sophistication as paralytic self-aware neurosis, the psychoanalyst's couch as quicksand. Generations of young Jewish men have striven to imitate the puncturing quippiness with which Allen carves out a space for himself in high society, perhaps missing the aggression in its barbed defensiveness.

Such idolization—no, romanticization—as exists in *Manhattan* is strictly backward-looking. As in the more savage *Husbands and Wives* (1992), released as his relationship with quasi-stepdaughter Soon-yi Previn became public, Allen plays a self-pitying middle-aged man drawn to a girl at the start of her life. In the final scenes of *Manhattan*, Isaac famously runs countless blocks, past fruit stands and park benches, to recapture his relationship with 17-going-on-18 Dalton student Tracy (Mariel Hemingway) before he loses her forever. It's a grand gesture; when he arrives, he's wheezing, so out of breath he looks liable to drop.

"We are all, in a sense, doomed," says *Metropolitan*'s Charlie Black (Taylor Nichols), as if the guillotine is sharpening for the UHB ("Urban Haute Bourgeoisie") and the film's Manhattan of hotel ballrooms and automats. Like Allen, writer-director Whit Stillman builds a whole teetering world out from his characters' high-class chatter. *Metropolitan* is set, per a title card, "not so long ago," at debutante balls and afterparties along old-money Park Avenue. Over winter break, the "Sally Fowler Rat Pack" gather at Sally's parents', discussing Austenian matters of

etiquette and sexual virtue, as well as the threat embodied thereto by the dread Rick Von Sloneker (Will Kempe) and his phallic ponytail.

Stillman based his first feature on his experiences as a shabby-genteel floater in this dimming WASPy milieu during the late 1960s. To emulate 30s-Hollywood elegance on a cash-poor budget, he made a product-placement deal with the 100-year-old formalwear store A.T. Harris; locations were donated by members of his cast and caste. Ex-deb Hundley's father lent his East 62nd Street townhouse, though the film's Fowler pad (where the actors napped on the floor during all-night shoots) was a mansion wrangled courtesy Stillman's distant relation Lew Lehrman, the 1982 Republican nominee for governor of New York.

Tom Townsend (Ed Clements) lives on the Upper West Side, near where Lincoln Center had recently risen over the Sharks and Jets' old stomping grounds. Like Stillman himself, he's been severed by divorce from his father's dynastic wealth, but still climbs the Ivy League circuit. Tom's outlook is a mix of romanticism and radicalism, but the latter barely puts up a fight, especially once an "escort shortage" sees him squiring the bookish Audrey Rouget (the Ringwaldian Carolyn Farina, who hailed from Queens, in contrast to fellow-actresses who've since appeared more frequently in the Weddings or Real Estate sections of the *Times* than in film reviews). Plus, as Nick Smith proclaims, "There's something a tiny bit arrogant about people going around feeling sorry for other people they consider less fortunate."

Played by Chris Eigeman, in his film debut, with purely Stillmanesque tones of sincerity and mischief, Nick is the most fully ensconced in the UHB (pronounced "uhb") bubble. It's not just that the dialogue resembles prose more than human speech—it resembles F. Scott Fitzgerald's prose, placing the script somewhere between autobiography and fond fantasy. "So many things which were better in the past have been abandoned for supposed convenience," says Nick.

Some Sally Fowler Rat Packers reappeared among the editorial assistants and rep-tie types in Stillman's *The Last Days of Disco* (1998), another film whose youthful characters feel preemptively nostalgic for the closing of a grace period. But *Metropolitan*'s chronological fuzziness is intentional, the passage of time marked not by historical events but by comforting seasonal rituals, like midnight mass at St. Thomas Episcopal, and Channel 11's annual Yule log video. As dawn approaches and the party breaks up, the characters hail cabs or walk home, overcoats bundled over today's fashions. The sky is leached of color, snow coats late-model cars and the new signage on old buildings, and you realize that New York at Christmastime is the closest any of us will ever get to time travel.

Central
Park North

110 st

96 st

Lexington
Av 53 St

MANHATTAN

CHAPTER
TWO
MIDTOWN

Flesh (Paul Morrissey, 1968) / *Midnight Cowboy* (John Schlesinger, 1969)

The opening crawl reads, "Andy Warhol presents *Flesh*"—specifically, the flesh of "Little Joe" Dallesandro, who, as Lou Reed sang in "Walk on the Wild Side," "never once gave it away." That's Joe, in a still from the film, on display on the cover of the first Smiths album, his abdominals in fat-free rolls as he sits up in bed, bangs covering what turns out to be a sharp, sensuous face, beatifically untroubled by the attention it attracts. In the opening scene, Joe's wife ties a bow around his erection, then sends him out onto the street to make money with it. In red bandana and tight Levi's, Joe loiters on the streetcorners Dee Dee Ramone wrote about in "53rd and 3rd." Yet in answer to the song's question about innocents used up by the New York skin trade—"Don't it make you feel sick?"—is Little Joe's wisdom imparted to a more squeamish fellow-hustler: "Nobody's straight, what's straight? [...] You just do whatever you have to do. [...] He's only gonna suck your peter, man."

Dallesandro was a juvenile delinquent who had been photographed for gay muscle mags like

Physique Pictorial. When he stumbled upon Warhol and Morrissey shooting *Loves of Ondine* (1967), they contrived a wrestling scene for him to appear in. *Flesh* opens with Joe face-down on his pillow, his mouth half-open, in a reference to Warhol's accurately titled 320-minute *Sleep* (1963). Though in color, featuring frequent camera movement and more developed dramatic situations, *Flesh*'s traces of amateurism—in-camera stop-start editing, raw sound, durational improvisation—are a link to Warhol's hands-off directing style. Warhol's films paid prescient, patience-trying attention to his "Superstars," the alternate-universe celebrities who hung out at the "Factory," Warhol's studio and a sort of Versailles court for speed freaks (located first on 47th Street and then around Union Square). *Flesh* sustains the Warholian alchemy of banality and exhibitionism, as Joe gets a blowjob while his fellow "Walk on the Wild Side" subjects, transgender Superstars Candy Darling and Jackie Curtis, read aloud from an old movie magazine.

Jonas Mekas, the film diarist, Anthology Film Archives co-founder and cheerleader-godfather of New York's underground and experimental film culture, had presented Warhol films at his roving Film-Makers' Cinematheque. In his *Village Voice*

"Movie Journal," he called *Flesh* "constructed, plotted, and executed with a definite calculation to keep one interested in it. [...] But a Warhol film never gives you an impression that it wants to make itself interesting."

Flesh came about when the makers of *Midnight Cowboy* recruited various Superstars for a party scene shot over a debauched week at Filmways Studio in Harlem. The scene was obviously inspired by Warhol's traveling show featuring the Velvet Underground and Nico—sporting sunglasses to protect their eyes from the psychedelic strobe lights and films projected onto the screen behind the stage. The "Up-Tight" performances hosted on Mekas's invitation at the Film-Makers' Cinematheque, then on 41st Street, were re-christened the "Exploding Plastic Inevitable" when they ran throughout April 1966 at a former German dance hall on St. Mark's Place (which beginning in 1967 was the hippie concert venue Electric Circus, and now claims as tenants a Chipotle and the punk clothing store Search and Destroy). In *Midnight Cowboy*, Superstar Viva plays the Super 8 filmmaker and party host; Morrissey made a film for the projections, though Warhol himself felt that "people with the money were taking the subject matter of the underground,

counterculture life and giving it a good, slick, commercial treatment." While recuperating from his near-assassination by radical feminist Valerie Solanas, Warhol suggested to Morrissey, his more technically ambitious collaborator, that his next film reclaim the territory.

John Schlesinger's X-rated *Midnight Cowboy* won Best Picture on the strength of its "subject matter of the underground, counterculture life." An archetypal New Hollywood shot would feature a man-on-the-street movie star barely picked out from the sidewalk throngs by a telephoto lens positioned blocks away. So when Dustin Hoffman's Ratso Rizzo stops in the crosswalk on 58th Street and 6th Avenue to pound the hood of the cab honking at him and shout, "I'm walkin' here!", it's pretty close to an artistic manifesto for an era of street-level storytelling.

It's also a New York thing—animalistic anger roused in a flash by a competitor for a precious sliver of real estate, and shaken off just as quickly—that makes city mouse Ratso a contrast with Jon Voight's fresh-off-the-bus Joe Buck. (Joe's the only one who stops when he sees a man in a business suit passed out on the sidewalk in front of Tiffany and Co.) Aspiring gigolo Joe checks into the Hotel Claridge over Times Square, where he poses for the mirror, not yet knowing that being one in a million means something different than it did in a small town. The film's experience of homelessness in a New York City winter is tactile, from the skin-chafing gray sky on down. Joe and Ratso shiver in a squat, smoking wet half-cigarettes and wrapping filthy blankets around clothes they haven't changed in days. (Costume designer Ann Roth found Ratso's white suit jacket in the garbage outside the Port Authority Bus Terminal.)

Under Mayor John Lindsay, New York's Office for Motion Pictures and Television streamlined the process for on-location shooting. "It's always in the headlines, whether it's the muggings or the arts," an assistant director on Schlesinger and Hoffman's *Marathon Man* (1976) told *New York Magazine*, in an article about the Lindsay location boom. "It's all here." As the classical Hollywood studio system disintegrated, the movies got to Lindsay's "Fun City" in time to mythologize it as a place of decline and decadence. Months before the *Midnight Cowboy* shoot, a nine-day sanitation strike left the city swamped in uncollected garbage, "as if it had finally become what we knew it was all along," per Margot Hentoff in the *Village Voice*.

The year after the Office was established, Vincent Canby, in the *New York Times*, pointed to the coming adaptation of *Midnight Cowboy* as evidence of the influence of Warhol's underground films. Despite (or because of) their treatments of gay life and drug use, they had emerged from alternative spaces to be regularly reviewed in the mainstream press, and compete for curious crowds with erotic Euro imports. At first, *Midnight Cowboy* is vaguer than James Leo Herlihy's source novel about the trauma that Joe Buck leaves behind in his hometown, and at once euphemistic and explicit about what he finds in the big city. Yet when Joe Buck looks at himself in the mirror and asks, in an echo of Little Joe's advice, "You know what you gotta do, cowboy?", it's as if the film is acknowledging that talking around the subject is superfluous. Joe Buck turns his trick with Bob Balaban, as a City College type in Coke-bottle glasses, in an old sci-fi movie playing on 42nd Street. Afterwards, the marquees along "the Deuce" suggest the progressive coarsening of the amusements then on offer: *The Thomas Crown Affair* (1968) at the Harris; Japanese creature feature *Frankenstein Conquers the World* (1965) at the Empire; the now-lost *The Twisted Sex* (1966) and *Justine* (1967), from New York-based nudie director Sande N. Johnsen, at the Liberty.

Amid Times Square's celebration of impersonal urban commerce—open-all-night neon, flashing billboards for whisky and Coke and deodorant—Joe and Ratso are lucky to have each other. In that, the film continues Warhol's legacy, not just anointing new culture icons, but celebrating their found families.

Taxi Driver (Martin Scorsese, 1976) / *Ms. 45* (Abel Ferrara, 1981) / *Variety* (Bette Gordon, 1983)

Taxi Driver begins with steam billowing upwards from a manhole cover, the sewer seeping into the streets. The film was shot as banks refused to further underwrite social services overextended across NYC's ever-poorer, ever less white population; during post production, President Ford—guided by advisers, including Donald Rumsfeld, determined to punish welfare-state profligacy—announced no federal bailout was forthcoming. The next day's *Daily News* front page read, "Ford to City: Drop Dead." In the summer of 1976, weeks after *Taxi Driver* won the Palme d'Or, David Berkowitz, the Son of Sam, began his .44 caliber killing spree. ("Hello from the gutters of N.Y.C. which are filled with dog manure, vomit, stale wine, urine and

blood," he wrote in a letter to *Daily News* columnist
Jimmy Breslin.) His capture came in August 1977, the
month after a 25-hour citywide blackout. In this city
on the brink, a cab emerges from the miasma like a
stage Satan in the parting of machine-made smoke—a
creature of the lower depths.

Taxi Driver screenwriter Paul Schrader, whose
Calvinist parents didn't let him go to the movies
growing up, had set out to be a minister, but changed
course after visiting the *New Yorker* film critic Pauline
Kael's apartment, talking film for hours and falling
asleep on her couch. Martin Scorsese was briefly
enrolled in a Catholic seminary, but found his vocation
in the secular cathedral of cinema. Cabbie Travis Bickle
"wandered in from the snowy wastelands of Michigan
to the fetid, overheated atmosphere of Marty's New
York," according to Schrader—or, in Travis's own
words, he's "God's lonely man."

Travis—who, like the city, never sleeps—trawls
42nd Street, past businessmen and bums and
hotpants hookers, the nocturnal city neo-noirish with
rain-slick tail lights, neon billboards and marquees.
(Like the NYPD's bygone baby-blue squad cars,
yellow taxi cabs are a pure pop of primary color in
the lurid palette of 70s New York.) The film parodies
the wise-cabbie trope popular with journalists

and politicians feigning a common touch. When patrician presidential candidate Charles Palantine hails Travis's cab, the hack tells him: "I don't follow political issues that closely, sir. [...] The President should just clean up this whole mess here. You should just flush it right down the fuckin' toilet."

There's something off about Travis, even before he begins bodybuilding and amassing a private arsenal. Like Al Pacino, the Ronaldo to his Messi, De Niro was a high school dropout who picked up the touchy idealism of Method acting at the Actors Studio, just as New Hollywood started sweeping up intense, weird-looking city-boy types to populate its scuzzy new locations. But while Pacino has played Richard III and Shylock, De Niro has steered clear of Shakespeare—maybe the characters are too lucid? Travis hits now-familiar pressure points from the hypersensitive De Niro-Scorsese filmography—his animal smirk from *Mean Streets* (1973), his boiling-blood destructiveness in *Raging Bull* (1980), and his pushy obliviousness from *The King of Comedy* (1982)—all united by the actor's does-this-guy-understand-himself? unpredictability.

His voiceover readings of Travis's mind-of-a-madman diary entries have a disconcerting banality. When Travis takes Palatine campaign worker Betsy (Cybill Shepherd) to see *Swedish Marriage Manual* at the Lyric on 42nd Street, she goes in with him, because she can't believe he doesn't have something up his sleeve beyond the barest conscious flicker of attraction and repulsion. As Travis loses himself in the pathology of the city, so does the film in Travis. Scorsese's cameo, as a fare with graphic plans to murder the wife who's cheating on him with a black man (the director uses another word), distills the twitchy, virulently hostile mindset.

In *New York Magazine*, film critic John Simon complained that "Travis seems hardly ever to drive through more prosperous neighborhoods"; the same issue featured as its cover story "The Siege of Fort Apache," by Captain Tom Walker, of the South Bronx's 41st Precinct. Walker opens on a scalping, and tells of

the battle to beat back the crime massing around the station house, "the last outpost" of civilization in the neighborhood. Joe Buck looked lost in Times Square in his fringed jacket and cowboy hat, suggesting, per Andrew Sarris in the *Village Voice*, "the satiric implications of the spectacle of a grown-up man still taking the Western myths of manhood seriously"—but it's no joke when Travis sets out to save 12-year-old prostitute Iris (Jodie Foster) from her pimp Sport (Harvey Keitel), like John Wayne dementedly chasing the Indian-abducted Natalie Wood in *The Searchers* (1956). Schrader wrote Sport as black, though Keitel was cast when the studio freaked out; when they meet, Travis wears cowboy boots, Sport wears a feather,

and the bloodbath that follows could be described, to borrow the title of Richard Slotkin's study of "the mythology of the American Frontier," as "regeneration through violence"—Travis taking his plea to Palantine into his own hands.

Before Travis Bickle, fellow civilian avenger Charles Bronson blasted away at New York's savages in *Death Wish* (1974)—the Urban Western could be as depraved as the fantasized city. After New York's near-bankruptcy, Mayor Abe Beame laid off thousands of municipal employees, including cops; in response, the police union distributed a "survival guide" called "Welcome to Fear City" at local airports, advising visitors to stay indoors and in terror. On the pamphlet's front page was a skull.

Another death's head: Thana (Zoë Tamerlis, later known as Zoë Lund), a young, beautiful, mute Garment District worker. She is raped first in an alley and then by a burglar in the opening minutes of *Ms. 45*, but finds her voice, as it were, shooting street harrassers, pickup artists and handsy bosses. Following his "video nasty" *The Driller Killer* (1979), Abel Ferrara found in the then-teenaged Lund the rare collaborator capable of matching his dark, wired energies. The two would reunite on *Bad Lieutenant* (1992), with Harvey Keitel acting out Ferrara's spiritual torment and addictive personality; the film's co-writer and, she claimed before her early death, co-director, Lund appears as a junkie (as she was) who shoots up Keitel. As Ms. 45, a silent-movie vamp with heavy eyebrows and cupid-bow lips, Lund is a reaction GIF *avant la lettre*, cuing Ferrara's most grossly exultant rubdown of the city's rancid underbelly. Even before Thana looks down the gunsight at her neighbor's dog, it's clear she won't stop at killing bad boys.

Ms. 45 emerged from the "fetid, overheated" grindhouse culture that *Taxi Driver* considers with fascination; *Variety*, in which a fair-haired girl from Michigan gets a job taking tickets at a porno theater, is about the theaters themselves, and suggests why this era is remembered so fondly.

The Variety Photoplay was actually on 3rd Avenue at East 13th Street. (Similarly, though Iris would have fit right in with the gum-smacking runaways of the "Minnesota Strip," on 8th Avenue by the Port Authority, it's the streets around the Variety that Sport's stable works.) A neighborhood nickelodeon dating from 1914, the Variety was by the final decade of its operation a second-run and porno theater where bums would sleep off a fortified-wine drunk, and the balcony was for cruising.

While Thana's outfits in *Ms. 45* grow increasingly sultry, culminating in a sexy-nun Halloween costume, *Variety*'s subversion of the male gaze is more interior. Christine (Sandy McLeod) stalks a patron through a smutty criminal underworld, pulled as if hypnotized into the dirty bookstores and peep shows around Times Square, booths glowing rosy-red like badly preserved celluloid. She delivers erotic monologues which her boyfriend finds confusing, and projects her fantasies onto the Variety screen.

Variety's kinky vibes come courtesy of John Lurie, of the No Wave act the Lounge Lizards, who did the suave, bleaty sax score; and through the script by cult writer Kathy Acker. Christine's friend Nan, who complains about not making any money from her photographs, is played by Nan Goldin, who was then embarking on her groundbreaking group-autobiographical photo project *The Ballad of Sexual Dependency*; Nan works, as Goldin did, at Tin Pan Alley, a 49th Street dive equally popular with starving artists and sex workers. *Variety* reflects back on the artistic and sexual liberation found in bottomed-out midtown— an implicit celebration of the explicit content, and behavior, by then on its way out.

New York's regeneration would come not through violence, but through private developers incentivized to rebuild the city in their own image, as described in Kim Pillips-Fein's book *Fear City*. Post-"Ford to City: Drop Dead," the young Donald Trump wrangled property-tax breaks to renovate 42nd Street's Commodore Hotel, now the Grand Hyatt (and shorted the city on rent). In the 1990s, the public-private "New 42nd Street" partnership saw some of *Midnight Cowboy* and *Taxi Driver*'s grandly decrepit grindhouses restored to first-run Broadway theaters via sweetheart deals to Disney: Bruce Ratner, later the developer of Brooklyn's Barclays Center, moved the Empire 170 feet toward 8th Avenue to serve as the lobby of the AMC Empire 25 multiplex, and demolished the Harris, where John Barrymore had played Hamlet, to bring in Madame Tussauds.

All That Jazz (Bob Fosse, 1979)

In Bob Fosse's *All that Jazz*, the wry, macho, Fosse-like director-choreographer Joe Gideon (Roy Scheider) prepares for his spectacular closing number, and reflects on a life in showbiz. Fosse had a heart attack while his Broadway show *Chicago* was in rehearsals and his Lenny Bruce biopic *Lenny* (1974) was in post-production; Joe's having chest pains as he works on his new musical, *NY/LA*, edits his film about a hip stand-up comic, and, in fantasy sequences with a Fellini-esque razzle-dazzle, flirts with death in the form of a white-veiled Jessica Lange (one of several Fosse flames in the cast).

The set pieces in *All That Jazz* roughly follow Fosse's career trajectory from stage to screen. *NY/LA*'s "Airotica" number, with its black hats, white gloves, cocked hips, rolling shoulders and leggy tempo, is the ultimate Fosse parody in its steamy amalgamation of camp, technique and sex appeal. Later production numbers on a bare soundstage culminate with a chorus line of showgirls, flipping their white feathered headdresses as if in one of Busby Berkeley's movie-magical 30s backstage musicals. Even the dance studios in the film, with their scuffed parquet floors, barre mirrors and exposed pipes, were replicated at Queens's recently reopened Astoria Studios.

So *All That Jazz* also tells a bigger story of "NY/LA" back-and-forth. Following Edison's development of the movie projector in New Jersey, film studios popped up all over New York, before going West to escape his patent claims—you can still see the Vitagraph smokestack in Midwood, Brooklyn. Paramount built Astoria Studios for its New York talent, like the Marx Brothers, who filmed their play *The Cocoanuts* (1929) there while simultaneously performing *Animal Crackers* on Broadway, then made the film of *Animal Crackers* (1930) there before joining the California gold rush. *All That Jazz* was shot a few years after the studio reopened, having latterly been used by the

Army for training films. (More recently, Alejandro González Iñárritu's *Birdman* [2014], a quite *All That Jazz*-y Broadway male melodrama, was shot there.)

As NYC feature-film production ground to a halt, the Depression also saw many Broadway theaters convert to moviehouses. When Fosse staged the musical *Sweet Charity* at the Palace Theatre, it marked the return of live entertainments to the former "Valhalla of Vaudeville" turned the RKO Palace, where *Citizen Kane* (1941) had its world premiere. (The Palace was rare in skipping the men-in-overcoats and teenagers-throwing-bottles-at-the-screen phase. As of this writing, the *Spongebob Squarepants* musical is playing at the Palace.) The Palace is also where, over seven days, Fosse filmed the *NY/LA* audition montage. The process mirrors Fosse's, with several dozen dancers going through the same motions at the same time, the director sending the unlucky ones home with a tap on the shoulder and a sympathetic, deadly-definite dismissal.

Several cameras covered the proceedings simultaneously, watching dancers stretching and putting on make-up, then leaping and spinning across the stage, their gym bags stacked in the wings. The accompanist plays on as the dancers accept Joe's verdicts with tearful brave little nods, or quick leaps of joy.

Set to "On Broadway," the sequence conjures up stock characters—dreamers, casting-couch fodder and seasoned wiseacres—and delivers behind-the-curtain cynicism in the little murmurings among Joe and the producers, but most of all, this is work. Fosse focuses on the routines and minutiae that show people would recognize as the common backdrop to their private dramas—even to his autobiographical extravaganza. These hopefuls have as much moxie as the hoofers of the Busby Berkeley-blessed *42nd Street* (1933) or the Gold Diggers movies, yet the suggestion here is of young people striving not for glory but for a gig.

Day Night Day Night
(Julia Loktev, 2006)

As I was writing this book, 27-year-old Brooklynite ISIS sympathizer Akayed Ullah detonated a pipe bomb strapped to his torso in the passageway connecting the 42nd Street/Port Authority and Times Square/42nd Street subway stops. Five people were injured, most seriously Ullah, whose stomach was charred by the blast. The bomb might have claimed several lives during a densely packed morning commute had its lone-wolf engineer assembled it properly.

Parents, not comprehending how infrequently their city-dwelling children go anywhere near Manhattan's postcard spots, are bound to worry about their precious ones being caught up in the headlines they read—never more so than during the George W. Bush years, when the Department of Homeland Security's five-level color-coded terror alert system was basically only ever set to yellow (paranoid) or orange (terrified). New Yorkers, fielding calls from Mom and Dad, or deflecting bloodthirsty political commentary, will never cop to fear, only to irritation at a disrupted commute. When New York instituted random subway bag checks after the 7/7 attacks in London, riders similarly understood the checks as security theater and a reminder of day-to-day life running on dumb luck.

In *Day Night Day Night*, a suicide bomber wanders through Times Square with an explosives-filled backpack. The film is as opaque as its title. In the first day and night, "She" prepares in a New Jersey motel. With her meek bearing and fierce dark eyes, Luisa Williams, in her sole feature-film role, projects unfathomable resolve within victimhood—Dreyer and Bresson's Joan of Arc films were a model.

In 2004, Bush was renominated during a Republican National Convention at Madison Square

Garden also marked by mass arrests of protestors on the streets of Midtown. War on Terror-era cinema was as politically contested as the post-9/11 image of New York City; Loktev, by contrast, effaces ideology entirely. Williams's She, like her American-accented handlers, is ethnically ambiguous. She murmurs prayers to an undefined "You," and her comically clumsy martyr video cuts out before her declaration.

On the second day and night, She emerges from the Port Authority with a yellow backpack. In *Day Night Day Night*'s urban vérité, the digital camera is nearly as unobtrusive as the nonprofessional star. It goes eye to eye with faces in the crowd, or catches darting close-ups of hands fiddling with phones. She is as ignored as any tourist or student with a too-heavy bag, and suddenly just as aimless, like she's too early to check in to her hotel. She waits to press the detonator button on her jerry-rigged MP3 player, first eating a mustard-slathered pretzel from a street vendor, then tearing into a candy apple. Her rationale—the reason why we might live or die—is totally remote to us.

The suspense is excruciating, but the film is not merely experiential, let alone exploitative. As Loktev told *New York Magazine*: "Any idiot can imagine why somebody might become a suicide bomber in

Times Square. We all read newspapers." *Day Night Day Night* refocuses on the individual level, imbuing terror with the same sense of mystery attached to every stranger on the sidewalk or the subway. City life is an act of faith.

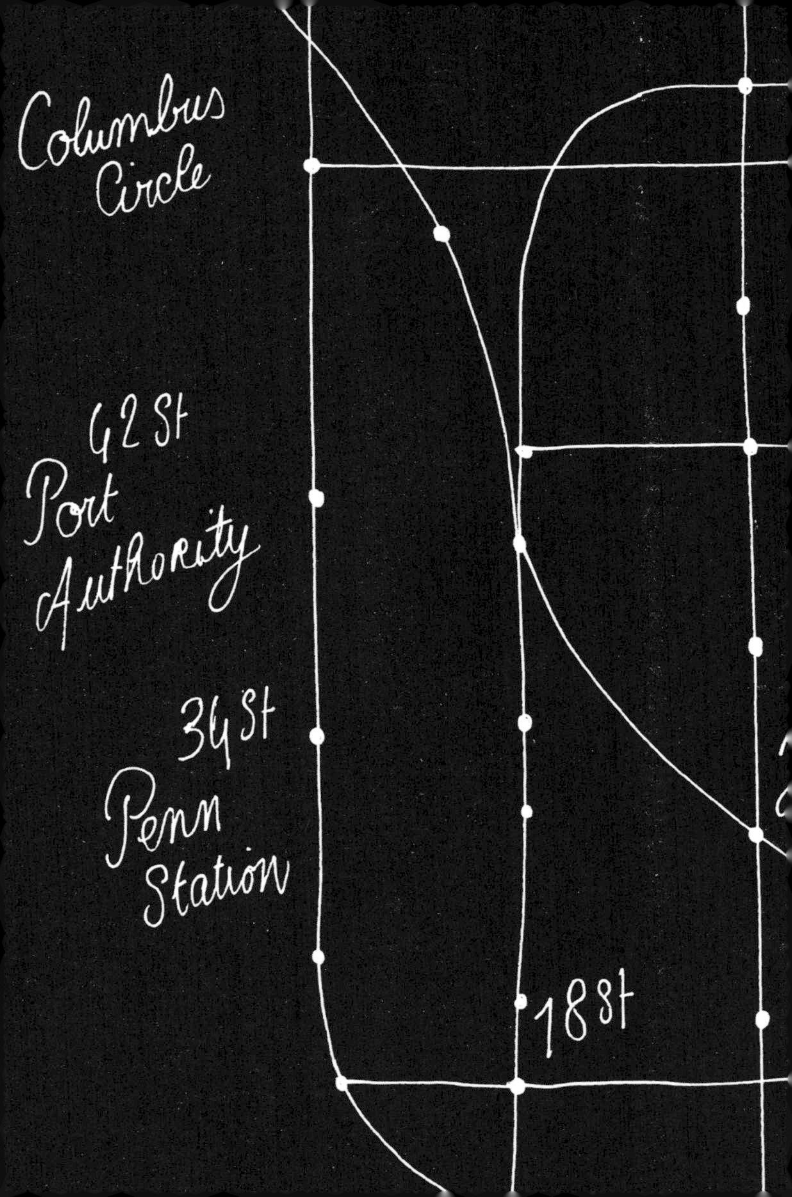

Columbus Circle

42 St
Port
Authority

34 St
Penn
Station

18 St

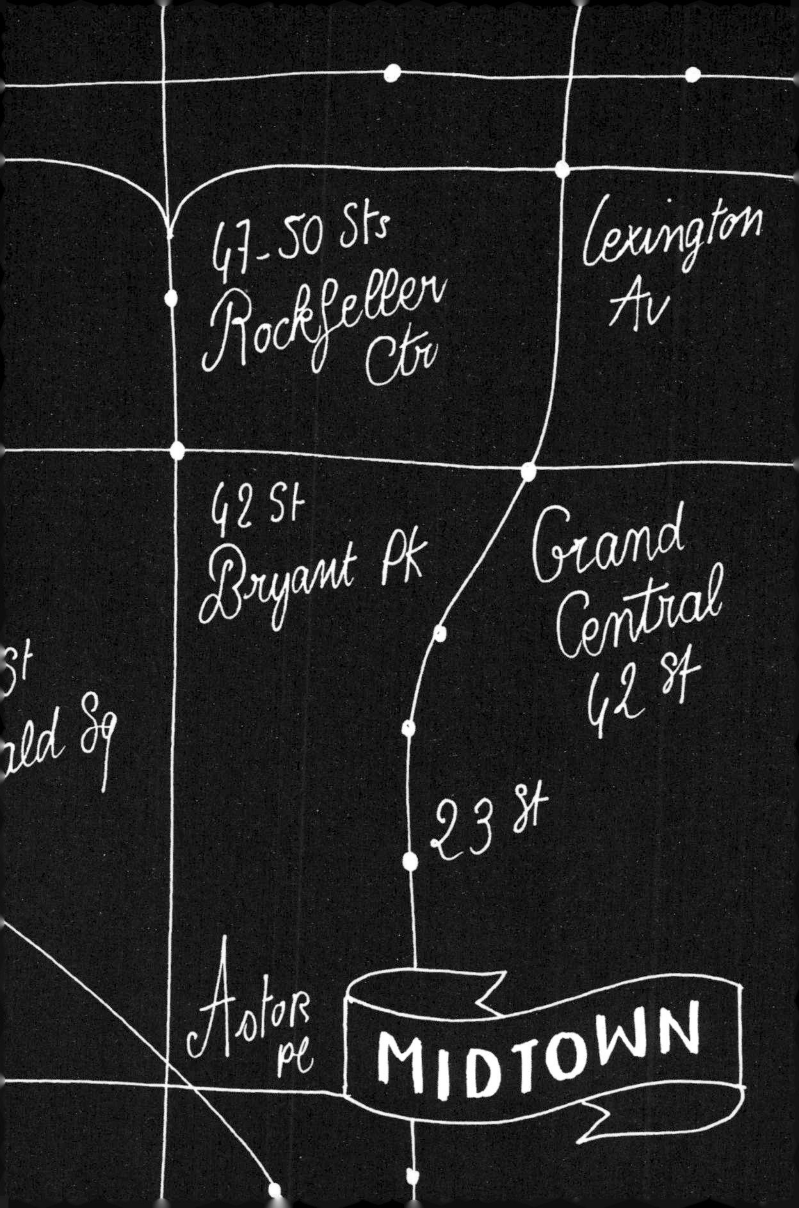

47-50 Sts
Rockefeller
Ctr

Lexington
Av

42 St
Bryant Pk

Grand
Central
42 St

St
ld Sq

23 St

Astor
Pl

MIDTOWN

CHAPTER
THREE
THE
VILLLAGES

Hi, Mom! (Brian De Palma, 1970)

I n 1918, a few years after taking lodgings at the Hotel Earle off Washington Square, the rising humorist P.G. Wodehouse collaborated with Guy Bolton and Jerome Kern on the musical *Oh, Lady! Lady!!*, including the song "Greenwich Village," to which Wodehouse's lyrics began:

> *Way down in Greenwich Village*
> *There's something, 'twould appear,*
> *Demoralizing in the atmosphere.*
> *Quite ordinary people,*
> *Who come to live down here,*
> *Get changed to perfect nuts within a year.*

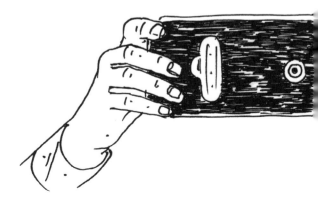

In *Hi, Mom!*, Brian De Palma and Robert De Niro shimmy to the latest youthquakes emanating from the Village's perpetual bohemia: out with the coffee-shop poets, folkies, and acid-washed longhairs, in with free love (and smut), experimental theater and radical politics. De Niro plays John Rubin, his character from De Palma's zany draft-dodger bro-down *Greetings* (1968), now a Vietnam veteran. This Peeping Tom moves in across Mercer Street from Silver Towers, the complex of three high-rises commissioned by NYU from I.M. Pei and completed in 1966. Like Jimmy Stewart in *Rear Window* (and like Craig Wasson in De Palma's high masterpiece *Body Double* [1984]), Rubin zooms in on the private lives of his neighbors: home movies, as it were, playing on the screen-shaped

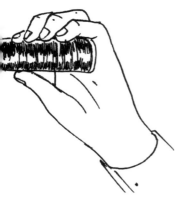

windows within Pei's gridded-concrete design. Unlike Jimmy Stewart, Rubin makes a play for Miss Lonelyhearts—but Judy (Jennifer Salt) proves more liberated than anticipated.

Through Judy's downstairs neighbor (Gerrit Graham), Rubin joins a revolutionary newsreel and theater collective's performance "Be Black, Baby." This sequence is in handheld black and white suggestive of the small-gauge celluloid records of the era's radical art and actions, like De Palma's film of the SoHo-based Performance Group's *Dionysus in '69* (1970). In it, a middle-class white audience are smeared with blackface make-up and then subjected to escalating terrorization by the whitefaced black performers, until the victims are regurgitated onto the street, and declare their agreement with the *New York Times*'s theater critic: that show was really something, so provocative. "Be Black, Baby" remains perhaps De Palma's most explosive exploration of spectatorship, fantasy and power, and a savage burlesque of the counterculture and its paying customers.

Greetings came out the year after the debut, at Lafayette Street's new Public Theater, of the hippie musical *Hair*. *Hi, Mom!* absorbs the influence of the violent upheavals of 1968, like the student-led occupation at De Palma's alma mater, Columbia

University—already reflected in Robert Kramer's *Ice* (1969), about armed rebellion and intra-left factionalism in a dystopian NYC. After *Hi, Mom!* was completed but two months before its release, three members of the white-kid activist army the Weather Underground—including Ted Gold, a leader of Columbia's antiwar movement—blew themselves up making a bomb at 18 West 11th Street. Writing a few weeks later in the *Village Voice*, left-wing journalist David Gelber reflected on "the acts of will by which [the Weather Underground] have undertaken to transform themselves into authentic guerillas" rather than "caricature[s] of the radical dilettante." By a similar act of will, filtered through De Niro's sociopath-next-door performance as one of Wodehouse's "perfect nuts," Rubin graduates from "Be Black, Baby" to bomb-plating anarchist.

With its plasticky commercial-jingle rock and soul soundtrack, *Hi, Mom!* imitates Jean-Luc Godard's sensibility, at once of and beyond pop culture (which, for in-the-know Village audiences, would also have included Godard movies). Andrew Sarris, reviewing the film in the *Voice*, proposed that "critics indulge movies like *Hi, Mom!* because they suspect that giddiness is the permanent life-style of the young, and that Out There is an undefined new sensibility stirring and why take a chance on missing it. Why not hedge by calling it a movie for audiences in Greenwich Village?" Way down in Greenwich Village, 'twould appear from *Hi, Mom!*, the hipsters try to outrun their influence over the culture at large, like Looney Tunes racing off a cliff without looking down.

The Foreigner (Amos Poe, 1978) / *Liquid Sky* (Slava Tsukerman, 1982)

Financed, an end-title card declares, "by a $5,000 personal loan from the Merchants Bank of New York," *The Foreigner* has all the cheapskate swagger of the CBGB's punk scene that birthed it. With Patti Smith's bandmate Ivan Král, Poe had directed the year-zero punk document *Blank Generation* (1976), featuring future icons trying on personas (dorky David Byrne, pouty Richard Hell) and tight jeans (the Ramones). *His Unmade Beds* (1976) was a jokey, poetic copy-of-a-copy remake of Godard's *Breathless* (1960), and *The Foreigner* was described by J. Hoberman in the *Village Voice* as an "attempt at a 'blank generation'

Alphaville [1965]". A plotless thriller, it's a parody in the way that punk was a parody of rock: the real thing, done by amateurs.

"Drifting across the Bowery," Hoberman wrote in a 1979 *Voice* feature on the "para-punk" cinema, "fallout from the 1977 punk 'explosion' continues to spawn art-world mutations. [...] these filmmakers parallel the music's energy, iconography, and aggressive anyone-can-do-it aesthetic, while using the performers themselves as a kind of ready-made pool of dramatic talent." Following Poe, filmmakers like Eric Mitchell, James Nares, Beth and Scott B and Vivienne Dick sprung up intertwined with punk music and artists like Nan Goldin. Recalling a previous generation's self-canonization and community-building, Hoberman continued, "the new underground's technically pragmatic films enact libidinal fantasies, parody mass cultural forms, [and] glorify a marginal lifestyle[.]" Mitchell's *Kidnapped* (1978) was "a poverty-row rehash of the [Warhol] Factory's assembly-line method"—as his *Underground U.S.A.* (1980) would remake *Flesh* with punks ready to make Superstars of each other.

Mitchell stars in *The Foreigner* as the bleach-blond, white-suited Max Menace, who lands at JFK, checks into the Hotel Chelsea—where Warhol shot

Chelsea Girls (1966) a decade before, and Nancy Spungen died a year later—and is the central figure in a conspiracy as all-encompassing and self-negating as in a Don DeLillo novel. The proudly slapdash film alternates passages of supreme ennui with skunky inventiveness. Who needs movie stars when you can ask Debbie Harry to bum a smoke and sing a German cabaret song direct-to-camera, like a back-alley Dietrich? The Cramps jump Max Menace in the grotty, graffiti-covered CBGB's bathroom; the camera shakes like crazy and the broad daylight blows out the exposure as Poe stages a one-car chase all over the neighborhood where DeLillo set his 1973 novel *Great Jones Street*, whose vision of rock's post-idealistic retreat into a void of violent refusal points the way to punk.

In *Liquid Sky*, another strange visitor orbits another outcast scene, a few blocks east and a few years later. Aliens have come to New York, in search of heroin: they're addicted to the neurochemical response, which is apparently similar to orgasm, and so also creep on copulating couples before delivering the ultimate high. (Their p.o.v. shots resemble the Predator's heat vision.) This is explained by a German scientist, to a hungry divorcée over Chinese takeout ("two orders of shrimp fried rice, an order of shrimp and pea pods, an order of shrimp with lobster sauce, and an order of jumbo shrimp"), as he stakes out the rooftop apartment where the UFO has landed.

Soviet émigré Slava Tsukerman—a foreigner, or perhaps an alien—co-wrote the film with Anne Carlisle, who stars as the model Margaret, and Margaret's nemesis, male model Jimmy. The two size each other up, narcissus-style; Margaret is Aladdin Sane, with harlequin make-up over a white base, and Jimmy is the Thin White Duke, with an electric-blond quiff and oversized tailored suits. The glam-camp gender-bending aesthetic is straight from the Pyramid Club on Avenue A, the real-life club where *Liquid Sky*'s models and dope fiends hang out. The Pyramid hosted performers like the space-age-pompadored go-go dancer John Sex, the young RuPaul, and Lady Bunny, who founded Wigstock, the annual drag festival in nearby Tompkins Square Park. (A subsequent film about aliens in Alphabet City, **batteries not included* [1987], in which space invaders save a tenement from demolition by a developer, anticipated the following year's Tompkins Square Park Riots, in which the NYPD clashed with the homeless, punks and squatters over a new curfew.)

Liquid Sky's Pyramid Club crowds dance to music recorded at the Public Access Synthesizer Studio, in

Pebbles and Bam-Bam animal prints, cat-eye glasses, or prom dresses and chokers—thrift-store Cinderellas like the young Madonna, then of East 4th Street and Avenue B. (Soon, the smash of "Like a Virgin" would draw crowds to the East Village shoot of *Desperately Seeking Susan* [1985], director Susan Seidelman's sunnier, studio-supported New Wave successor to her hand-to-mouth punk debut *Smithereens* [1982].) "I was taught that I should come to New York, become an independent woman," Margaret says in a late-movie monologue, tempted by the alien promise of hedonistic oblivion. The overlapping East Village scenes of *The Foreigner* and *Liquid Sky* produced many stars—but these were themselves produced by the uncanonized fabulousness of even more Margarets.

Cruising (William Friedkin, 1980) / *How to Be Single* (Christian Ditter, 2016)

A murderer stalks the city's gay leather scene, and rookie cop Steve Burns (Al Pacino) goes undercover to draw the killer out. Released by Universal onto more than 500 screens nationwide, *Cruising* doesn't exactly illuminate its subject: as pale, permed Pacino crawls clubs and curbs among the meatpacking plants by the piers on Manhattan's far west side, Steve is soon too deep into an underworld rendered dungeon-like in steel-blue light.

Inspired by the gay activist and *Village Voice* journalist Arthur Bell, New York's queer community disrupted *Cruising*'s production in the summer of 1979—most of the film's live-recorded dialogue was unusable for the jeers and whistles from crowds gathered out-of-frame. The film "promises to be the most oppressive, ugly, bigoted look at homosexuality ever presented on the screen, the worst possible nightmare for the most uptight straight," Bell had written. His beat covered the gay rights struggle, as well as crime within the queer community, including the killings that inspired *Cruising*. In January of 1977, his *Voice* essay "Looking for Mr. Gaybar" considered liberation, libertinism and the "Death Wish" of the backroom-bar scene in the years following the Stonewall riots. At the Mineshaft, where Robert Mapplethorpe, famous for his BDSM-themed photographs, was a regular, Bell described seeing: "a long-haired gentleman stretched and strung. Cries of ecstasy leave his lips as the passing parade sticks hands, wrists, elbows up his rectum." Later that year, Bell reported that the Mineshaft was among the bars

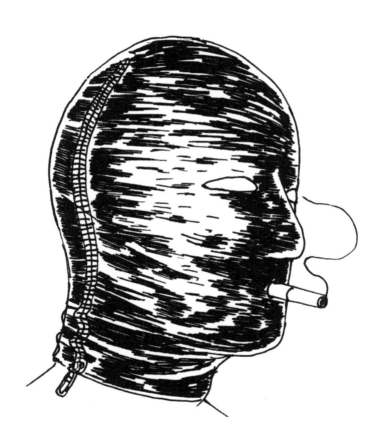

visited by the *Variety* film critic Addison Verrill on the night of his murder by a stranger he'd picked up. The killer then called Bell to confess; his name was Paul Bateson, and in his daytime life as an X-Ray tech at NYU Medical Center, he'd appeared in a hospital scene of William Friedkin's *The Exorcist* (1973).

Both Pacino and Friedkin went to the Mineshaft for research—Friedkin on "jockstrap night"—but Mineshaft manager Wally Wallace would only let members like Mapplethorpe take photos inside. *Cruising*'s "Cockpit" scenes were filmed a block away at Hellfire; Friedkin rented the adjacent industrial space on Washington Street between West 13th and Little West 12th in order to film entrances and exits around the cobblestones and loading bays, complete with dangling meathooks. The Mineshaft was, despite its name, upstairs from street level; Steve Burns goes down, down, down.

The apartment Steve moves into, on Jones Street, is around the corner from Pacino's Minetta Street basement pad in *Serpico* (1973); as in the previous film, the actor takes in downtown's tree of knowledge with his natural engine-revving watchfulness. Steve is initially confounded by the sexual come-ons encoded in everyone's choice of handkerchief, but eventually takes poppers, is bound while nude, and gets picked up in Central Park. In *Cruising* as in the grungy, nihilistic *The French Connection* (1971), his previous New York policier, Friedkin zeroes on the prurient with blank-faced detachment. Many of the Cockpit extras were Mineshaft patrons: sweating in leather jackets or full pelts over untanned torsos, they fill the frame, licking boots, or lubing an arm up to the elbow with Crisco. Friedkin rotates multiple actors through the roles of killer and victim in the murder scenes, while also leaving open the possibility that Steve has committed at least one murder out of self-loathing homophobia, and suggesting that the killer—or a killer—is still at large. The ambiguity underscores a metaphor of contagion, which takes on a tragic prescience given what would happen to so many of the men dancing in the Cockpit.

In "Looking for Mr. Gaybar," Bell warned vulnerable peers about self-destructive behavior, noting that "gay-style murders" were usually unreported and unsolved. (Early in *Cruising*, closet-case cops abuse trans sex workers.) He was also protective of their image; to him, if not to *Cruising*'s extras, Friedkin's film painted gay sexuality as deviant, dangerous, a cause beyond the political pale. But three decades after AIDS forced the closure of the Mineshaft, another *Voice* writer, film critic Nathan Lee, could call the reissued *Cruising* "a heady, horny flashback to the last gasp of full-blown sexual abandon."

Another horny epoch graced the West Village and Meatpacking District in the summer of 2000, when *Sex and the City* sent Samantha to live on West 13th, and Carrie and Miranda to eat cupcakes at the Magnolia Bakery on Bleecker and West 11th. Always aspirational, demanding thicker skins and sharper wits than America's soft middle, the New York lifestyle post-*SATC* promised exceptionalism for the cost of an HBO subscription (much more affordable if your parents are helping with the rent).

The bar where *How to Be Single*'s Alice (Dakota Johnson) hangs out is on Gansvoort Street, a block from the old Mineshaft, and also now from the High Line, the abandoned elevated railroad spur turned promenade past boutique retail, bottle-service clubs and luxury hotels. (The bar's long metal awning nods to the neighborhood's industrial past—no more meathooks, though.) Fresh out of college, Alice cabs it over the Manhattan Bridge, head out the window Kevin McCallister-style, while the soundtrack plays Taylor Swift's "Welcome to New York". Cruising-wise, Alice starts out as naïve as Pacino with his yellow handkerchief, though both sex, and the city, are safer now than ever. With its wikihow title and awareness of rom-com convention, *How to Be Single* is a film about a privileged young person's journey of self-discovery down a trail blazed by more marginal people—an authentic New York story, if we're honest.

When Harry Met Sally (Rob Reiner, 1989)

Nora Ephron's romantic comedies explore the wit and foibles of characters with an above-average complement of both—well-off, frazzled people, who acknowledge everyday obstacles with hysterical panache, like the frizzy-haired characters of *New Yorker* cartoonist Roz Chast.

In Ephron's breakthrough script, Meg Ryan and Billy Crystal play friends who spend decades falling into each other's arms without knowing it, punctuated by one moment of private experience made brazenly public. It happens in Katz's Delicatessen, on East Houston and Ludlow Streets, a Jewish sandwich shop opened in 1888 whose period-friendly fittings and fixings, pressed tin and pastrami, have made it a frequent film location. Katz's is also a monument to

the Lower East Side's years as a Jewish slum, a period memorialized by Budd Schulberg in *What Makes Sammy Run?* as a place that bred fast talkers, unself-conscious and pushy. So Katz's is the perfect place for Ryan's Sally to prove that there's more to her than her blonde perm and an overwhelming impression of prudishness. When Crystal's Harry dismissively feeds Sally some man-of-the-world nonsense about his superior sexual acumen, Sally retorts by mimicking a full-scale screaming orgasm, from moans to hair-tossing to table-pounding and back again, all to Harry's mortification and her fellow diners' blank-faced bemusement. Sally shows that she's not some heartland ditz, but capable of being as frank, as funny, and as unselfconsciously loud as anyone. Standup comedian David Cross has joked that, "In New York, you are constantly faced with this very urgent decision that you have to make, about every twenty minutes [...] 'Do I look at the most beautiful woman in the world or the craziest guy in the world?'" For one glorious moment over a tower of cold cuts, the hot chick and crazy person are one and the same.

Kids (Larry Clark, 1995)

Over the single summer day and night of photographer Larry Clark's first film—the subject of a ratings battle, concerns of child-pornography charges, intense parent-child conversations, stratospheric praise and rabid criticism—the kids of *Kids* indulge in teen-rebellion universals, like shoplifting from a bodega, and breaking into the Carmine Street swimming pool after hours. They also drink malt liquor on the street and piss it out on the sidewalk, mob together to beat up a bystander in the park, and aggressively pursue unprotected sex, which they talk about with an explicitness at odds with both their age, and the specter of AIDS that haunts the film. Telly (Leo Fitzpatrick), the "virgin surgeon," is HIV-positive, but doesn't know it; in the film's first scene, he cajoles a very young-looking girl into her first, painful sexual experience, telling her how beautiful she is, and immediately afterwards telling his friend Casper (Justin Pierce) to smell his fingers.

Clark developed the film by hanging out in Washington Square Park and at the new Supreme shop with skateboarders whose father he was old enough to be (and for whom he'd sometimes buy booze). Though he got himself a skateboard ("the image on

the board is a naked young girl bent at the waist," *New York Magazine* reported in their cover story, "her rear in the air and her vagina exposed. She appears to be winking at the camera"), he's not particularly interested in skating. Mostly Clark likes watching groups of kids in public, doing the occasional kickflip like a masturbatory reflex but mostly just spread out across the lip of the park's fountain like a slouchy wolfpack, passing around a blunt (rolled with real weed, and, if you believe what the characters say, the rare good bud ever purchased in Washington Square Park). Casper, especially, speaks in snotty, growly hip-hop-inflected slang, a reflection of the mixed-race city that produced rap groups like the Beastie Boys and A Tribe Called Quest, featured on the soundtrack and finally rewiring adolescent brains nationwide. (City kids grow up in public—their parents' apartments are so small—and it's how they've grown up so much faster than their suburban peers, in matters from race to sex.)

Clark had met NYU screenwriting prodigy Harmony Korine in Washington Square Park, too, and gave him a story prompt to fill out on his own; most cast members have since said that the incidents in the film are compressed and heightened, but basically familiar from their own wild-child experiences. The cast was found on the street—like Rosario Dawson, spotted on a stoop—and through Clark's skate kids' friends, and friends of friends. Korine knew Pierce from his skating days, as well as Harold Hunter, who grew up in the projects in the East Village and had toured with the Zoo York crew for several years, and Chloë Sevigny, the "It Girl" of downtown fashion magazines like *Paper* and *Sassy*. She plays Jenny, previously "devirginzied" by Telly, who gets her test results early in the movie and spends the rest of it trying to track him down.

Shot handheld, with natural light, the film's look is pervy and rhapsodic, the camera taking in the hairless, stretched-taffy torsos of boys from 12 to 20 as they despoil themselves, naturally beautiful but also coughing, giggling, puking, getting droopy-eyed with drink and drugs they have no tolerance for. But despite the candid camerawork, word-slurring non-actors and raw-dog content, this really is the movie version, the one where a pretty white girl from a good home gets HIV the first time she has sex. Embellishing Clark's "maiden-tied-to-the-tracks" plot hook with his own firecracker-under-the-porch imagination, Korine also shows off an advanced sense of structure. The frequent editorializing cross-cuts and soundtrack choices make it hard to tell how "real" the behavior is—and it's perhaps that uncertainty, as much as the shock of the film, that gave *Kids* authority as a portrait of inscrutable youth. With Fitzpatrick's undropped, novocaine-numb voice, full of "likes" an' shit, Telly sounds like one of those loud kids on the subway who's completely oblivious to how he appears to the adults going to work. Still, subsequent generations of New York-native kids have grown up in thrall to the film's attitude of dirtbag diffidence. To a young viewer, *Kids* is assuredly a cautionary tale, but it's also a particularly New York fantasy of adolescent autonomy: no trade-off between mobility and adult supervision!

8 Av

23 St

Christopher St
Sheridan Sq

Wl
Wa

Houston
St

14 St Union

Sq

Bleecker St

Delancey St
Essex St

ce
t

THE VILLAGES

CHAPTER
FOUR
LOWER
MANHATTAN

King Kong (John Guillermin, 1976)

I n March 1933, as 10,000 cinemagoers at Radio City Music Hall and the RKO Roxy watched a stop-motion King Kong swat at biplanes atop a model of the Empire State Building, two 20th century legends were born: of the first larger-than-life, man-made movie myth, and of the world's tallest building, opened two years before.

King Kong appropriately climaxed on the skyscraper whose metallic opulence was the literal pinnacle of the Art Deco aesthetic beloved by classical Hollywood's set dressers. Four decades later, during the eras of corporate-conglomerate blockbusters and brutalist urban planning, super-producer Dino De Laurentiis announced his bicentennial-year *King Kong* remake with full-color ads showing Kong astride the Twin Towers of the World Trade Center, the city's newly crowned summit.

The film's World Trade Center shots were filmed over two nights in the summer of '76. *Kong* was assembled flat-pack style in the plaza between the North and South towers. The first night, a couple thousand unpaid New Yorkers gathered, many breaking through a ring of paid extras to clamber over the great ape, yanking out locks of Argentinean

horsehair for souvenirs. The second night, 30,000 people showed up.

King Kong was among the top box-office attractions of 1976, though many felt as the *New York Times*'s Vincent Canby, who called the film "inoffensive, uncomplicated fun," and added: "One of my objections to the film is the substitution of the twin towers of the Trade Center for the Empire State Building [...] The World Trade Center is a very boring piece of architecture. The Empire State Building is not."

The WTC was one of postwar New York's most dubious urban-renewal projects, like the highways and high-rises of "master builder" Robert Moses. A whole neighborhood known as Radio Row was razed to make way for widened arterial roads and the 16-acre WTC "superblock." Architecture critic Lewis Mumford described the massive concrete towers as "a characteristic example of the purposeless giantism and technological exhibitionism that are now eviscerating the living tissue of every great city."

The movies soon lost interest in the Twin Towers. They've served as an orientation point in countless establishing shots, and been blown up in disaster movies that flaunt their power to reshape the world. But never again were the towers showcased like they are here, when Kong's blonde bride Jessica

Lange screams as the dying Kong slams an Army helicopter into the side of one of the towers.

Reviewing *King Kong, Time Magazine*'s Richard Shickel observed that, after escaping the chains of his oil-company masters, Kong's "final destructive binge could be seen [...] as a projection of Western fears of, what might happen if the Third World should develop its potential power and strike back." The resonance has only deepened since. Stills from the WTC attack in *Super Mario Brothers* (1993) are sometime circulated amongst 9/11 truthers; characters flee Lower Manhattan in terror and confusion after the decapitation of the Statue of Liberty in *Cloverfield* (2008), which arguably mainlines more 9/11 trauma than Oliver Stone's *World Trade Center* (2006), shot primarily at a respectful distance in Los Angeles. The Twin Towers have become more conspicuous on film now that their absence is one of the defining aspects of American life.

Sleepwalk (Sara Driver, 1986)

SoHo after dark, in *Sleepwalk*, is as depopulated as an Edward Hopper painting, but quavering with dread. From directly overhead, street lamps illuminate tableaux of uncollected garbage, street numbers spray painted onto fire-stair doors, metal shutters shielding unknown storefronts, all amplifying the cold echo of footsteps. Nighttime south of Houston Street was then, by reputation at least, somewhere and -when anything might happen, deserted as the neighborhood was by all but freaks drawn to cheap rents. In *Sleepwalk* the implications are less bohemian than mystical.

In Martin Scorsese's *After Hours* (1985), office drone Griffin Dunne is ingested and regurgitated by SoHo after an odyssey of sexual frustration and financial humiliation. It's a tourist's view of a scene that was by then notorious enough to have been acknowledged at Cannes, when Jim Jarmusch won the Camera d'Or for *Stranger Than Paradise* (1984). Jarmusch's film is funnier than *After Hours*, if you can hear the jokes through the dead air; hungry-looking musicians John Lurie and Richard Edson (Sonic Youth's original drummer), and Hungarian-born Eszter Balint, of the storefront Squat Theater, feel less like actors than acquaintances who happened to be hanging out while the camera was running.

Jarmusch was the camera operator for *Sleepwalk*, co-written and directed by his NYU film school classmate and long-term romantic partner Sara

Driver, whose brief, vivid filmography vibrates to a frequency all but inaudible to uptown ears. *Sleepwalk* is aptly titled, turned on to the French Symbolist poetry beloved by CBGB's waifs like Patti Smith and Tom Verlaine. Suzanne Fletcher, seen briefly in *Variety* and throughout *The Ballad of Sexual Dependency*, plays Nicole, a single mother, print-shop toiler and Mandarin speaker commissioned by the sinister "Dr. Gou" and his long-fingered assistant (Tony Todd!) to translate an ancient scroll. Over several sticky-asphalt summer nights, the text bleeds spookily into her life.

In 2012, Driver told the *Village Voice*'s Nick Pinkerton of her interest in the subconscious, and described *Sleepwalk* as a downtown diary: "New York was such an emotional place at that time; you were very sensitive to stuff on the streets. [...] I kept a journal of weird things that happened to me on the street, which I incorporated into *Sleepwalk*." The production featured several historically significant hipsters: Steve Buscemi is fussy and funny as Nicole's officemate; performance artist Ann Magnuson is French-accented and funny as her roommate. But it primarily evokes a private headspace, as Nicole's nightly perambulations take her past feral businessmen and lost children, sentient objects and apparitions. "We found all our furniture on Tuesday nights out on the streets," Driver recalled. "I remember seeing Louise Nevelson, the sculptor, on Mott Street. She was looking for pieces of wood in the garbage. She had these mink eyelashes on, and it was raining. One was drooping ..."

Nicole's print shop is on Crosby Street, directly south of Houston. One block east on Lafayette is the Puck Building, the former offices of *Puck* and *Spy*, satirical magazines for two Gilded Ages, and where Harry confessed his love to Sally. It's now a luxury condo conversion courtesy of second-generation real-estate schemer turned presidential consigliere Jared Kushner. One block west is a Hollister, a Victoria's Secret and a Forever 21. We can wonder how the world would be different if Driver had had the opportunity to be as prolific as Jarmusch, but it's fitting we only catch the occasional glimpse of her ghostly New York.

Wall Street (Oliver Stone, 1987) / *Working Girl* (Mike Nichols, 1988)

On the morning of December 15, 1989, an 18-foot, 7,000-pound bronze statue of a bull—muscles rippling, nostrils flaring—was discovered outside the New York Stock Exchange. Sicilian-born sculptor Arturo Di Modica deposited his "Charging Bull" in front of the spiritual home of global commerce, he said, in tribute to "the strength and power of the American people." Over the years, tourists have burnished the bull's testicles to a golden shine, though it was hard to reach during 2011's Occupy Wall Street protests, as the NYPD kept watch against symbolically potent vandalism.

Wall Street is full of charging bulls—in his oleaginous Oscar-clip "Greed is good" speech, Michael Douglas's corporate raider Gordon Gekko posits his

personal brand of stock-market swashbuckling as a recipe for Making America Great Again. Too, there is stockbroker Bud Fox (Charlie Sheen), a class-climbing NYU grad still reliant on cash handouts from his mechanic father to support his high-turnover lifestyle. Bud's naïve materialism slides frictionlessly into amorality as he ascends from bottled lagers at a Queens tavern with his dad's union buddies, to a yuppie-paradise penthouse with a sushi machine, though he pays more attention to the Bloomberg terminal at his desk than to the Schnabel canvas on his wall. Stone's trading montages unspool in a headrush of scrolling stock tickers, brokers barking buy and sell orders, and floor traders in frantic open-outcry bidding. The film is set in 1985, during the Reagan bull market, when Donald Trump was but a gold-plated mascot of trickle-down economics. It's dedicated to Stone's stockbroker father, who died that same year; paternal bonds and the Protestant work ethic are the moral compass buried under a Gatsby-esque pile of baby-blue contrast-collar shirts.

In March 2017, "Charging Bull" was joined at Bowling Green Park by the four-foot-two "Fearless Girl," who faces the bull with her hands on her hips and head thrown proudly back. Following the inauguration of the suddenly sinister Naugahyde

Göring, "Fearless Girl"'s fresh-faced defiance of the bull's rampage, and her ubiquity in selfies and memes, seemed to speak to the righteous, affirming ideal form of #resistance. "Fearless Girl" was commissioned by McCann, one of the world's largest advertising firms, as part of a corporate PR campaign for the investment firm State Street Global Advisors.

In contrast to all the unbridled testosterone of *Wall Street*, *Working Girl* offers up a plucky underdog heroine, for a cuddlier story of corporate capitalism. The movie's very own "Fearless Girl" is Tess McGill (Melanie Griffith), who, like Bud Fox, is an outerborough striver, in this case from Staten Island. (The borough is personified by her meathead boyfriend Alec Baldwin, who, with his furry chest, slicked-back hair, nautical tattoo and pretty-boy pout, looks like the star of a gay-for-pay porn parody of the entire Billy Joel catalog.) Tess rides the ferry to work in the Financial District, and her morning commute is practically an immigrant epic, with the camera swooping past the Statue of Liberty and the Manhattan skyline glittering like a fortress before her. Self-trained swot Tess is overlooked by her chauvinistic colleagues—like *Wall Street*, *Working Girl* features a scene where its protagonist is offered champagne and cocaine in the back of a limo, though here it's proffered not by a high-class call girl but by a handsy Kevin Spacey. New boss Katherine (Sigourney Weaver) is a proto-*Lean In* success story whose lip-service feminism foreshadows her duplicity.

Working Girl is a Cinderella story with boardrooms for ballrooms, and the same imposter syndrome to get over. Like Bud, Tess lives a double life as entry-level worker bee and incognito dealmaker, brokering a media merger with a white-collar Prince Charming (Harrison Ford) enlisted from her boss's Rolodex.

When Tess gatecrashes a society wedding to make a pitch, it feels less realistic than the rapid-fire arcana of *Wall Street*, more like something in screwball comedy. Yet Bud, too, demonstrates his initiative not by crunching numbers but by stalking one of Gekko's business rivals on a motorcycle. The prize company in *Working Girl* is a radio station; in *Wall Street* it's budget airlines and steel and paper mills—all quaint, now that wealth is increasingly generated by exotic derivative products, and stock trading increasingly dominated by algorithm-driven high-frequency trading out of vast server banks in New Jersey. Both *Wall Street* and *Working Girl* are nostalgic in their emphasis on the human element. High finance is still an arena for individual will, rather than the faceless, placeless elite protested by Occupy Wall Street.

Tiny Furniture (Lena Dunham, 2010) / *Girlfriends* (Claudia Weill, 1978)

Tiny Furniture's release, months after Lena Dunham's 24th birthday, was heralded by a *New Yorker* profile making matter-of-fact reference to "Dunham's

generation," and commensurate backlash contesting the universality of a rich white girl's navel-gazing. The debate rages on. But though Dunham owes at least something of her stature to being first past the post at metabolizing millennial experience, to watch *Tiny Furniture* now is to see not just an artist who's a work-in-progress, but a demographic as well.

Dunham plays Aura, recently graduated from Oberlin, dumped by her boyfriend and boomeranging back to her childhood bedroom in her family's Tribeca loft (where Dunham indeed returned after breaking

up with her college boyfriend). There she mopes, oversleeps, and snipes with her artist mother Siri (played by Dunham's mother, photographer Laurie Simmons) and her high-achieving sister Nadine (played by Dunham's sister Grace, then an award-winning teen poet). Dunham wrote and shot *Tiny Furniture* over less than a month in October and November of 2009. When did she have time to feel inertia? She graduated from Oberlin in spring 2008, and was at SXSW in spring 2009 with her first feature, *Creative Nonfiction*.

At SXSW '09, Dunham met Alex Karpovsky, who here plays the YouTube personality "The Nietzschean Cowboy," and others associated with mumblecore—a quickly exhausted descriptor for a genre of microbudget films launched at SXSW and other regional festivals, whose shabby-edged visuals, no-filter nudity and ah, um ... dialogue give the sense of films worked through on the fly as their young characters work through quarterlife-adjacent uncertainties. Cramped apartments in Williamsburg, in Andrew Bujalski's *Mutual Appreciation* (2005), and Park Slope, in Aaron Katz's *Quiet City* (2007), had previously hosted Dunham's cinematic older siblings. *Tiny Furniture* was mumblecore with crossover appeal, building scenes to hammer-drop punchlines ("My heart is broken, and my vagina hurts so much!"). It feels significant that Aura and The Nietzschean Cowboy blow off a subtitled movie at Film Forum, the arthouse cinema a few blocks from Dunham's house.

Dunham's crowd-pleasing instincts spring from the same generational traits her film explores. Aura trains her personality to friends and prospective lovers, and bares her body and her anxieties, to the extent that they're separate, with a mix of defiance, self-loathing and neediness that's always contingent on an audience. Yet the millennials of *Tiny Furniture* flirt via MySpace, not Tinder, and take meetings with Comedy Central, rather than monetize their Snapchat platform. Dunham's zeitgeist-bottling HBO sitcom *Girls* proffers a more articulated generational portrait, with Dunham's avatar made into a Brooklyn transplant whose Midwestern parents fund their special-snowflake daughter's ambiguously liberal-artistic ambitions; *Tiny Furniture* is a Manhattan home movie. The Dunham loft at 16 Desbrosses Street was a former warehouse purchased and converted to working and living space by downtown artists, most of whom have since sold on at a tidy profit; shot in widescreen, it's 3600 square feet of white walls and modular shelving, embodying a chic, intellectually forbidding birthright.

The title *Tiny Furniture* refers to Siri's work in the film, represented by the staged photographs of dollhouse furnishings with which Laurie Simmons really did make her name, as a member of the post-Pop Art channel surfers in the so-called Pictures Generation. By extension, it suggests Aura's inchoate drive to make meaningful art of her own. In the film's most affecting thread, Aura finds her mother's diary—again, a real-life family artifact—from her days as an unknown photographer in the 1970s SoHo gallery scene. Like mother, like daughter: daffy insecurities about food and boys mingle with sincere yearning to do good work.

The funk of uncertainty and the euphoria of affirmation, and the similar-but-different milieu in which Laurie Simmons experienced them a generation before her daughter, are concerns of Claudia Weill's *Girlfriends*, a favorite film of Dunham's. The apartments in *Girlfriends*, with paint and plaster over old wiring and keyholes, feel like analogue versions of *Tiny Furniture*'s white-cube loft.

As photographer Susan Weinblatt, Melanie Mayron has the full-on presence of an aspiring artist blundering through established art-world and social conventions. Susan, like Aura, cycles through diffident or unsuitable boys, but her real partner is her roommate Anne (Anita Skinner), who reads her poetry to Susan through the bathroom door. Anne's fade into domesticity with Martin (Bob Balaban) occasions a mutual identity crisis; when Anne and Martin show Susan their honeymoon slides and unintentionally cycle through a candid of Bob's bare Balabuns, it's not just a proto-Lena Dunham moment of light mortification, it's like Susan is receiving photographic confirmation that Anne is cheating on her, and a spur to rethink her relationships and her identity.

Girlfriends has the quizzical air of the Ann Beattie stories then appearing in the *New Yorker*, sketches of postcollegiate anomie that were greeted in some quarters as reports on a "Beattie Generation." Really, though, as in *Girlfriends* and *Tiny Furniture*, the quirks of the artist's hard-won sensibility are a million times more interesting.

Houston St

Park
Palace

World Trade
Center

Rector
St

Prince St
East Broadway
nal St
lton
Broad St
LOWER MANHATTAN
th Ferry

CHAPTER FIVE
UPTOWN AND THE BRONX

The Cool World (Shirley Clarke, 1963) / *Gloria* (John Cassavetes, 1980)

The first feature film shot on location in Harlem, *The Cool World* is perspective-upending in more than just its teen-gang plot. Fourteen-year-old Duke (Hampton Clanton) dreams of being a "cool killer," the "biggest man on the street," by obtaining a gun—a "piece," in the film's anthropologically on-point dialog. Throughout the film, Clarke also takes a lively, intent interest in the lives surrounding Duke's sordid coming-of-age—an update of Helen Levitt, Janice Loeb and James Agee's groundbreaking short documentary *In the Street* (1948), also shot in Harlem. Old ladies push grocery carts and kids in canvas sneakers and cardigans smoke stubby cigarettes; street vendors sell boosted merchandise out of sight of the cops—the forbears of today's peddlers of loosies, bootleg DVDs, and "nutcracker" spiked fruit cocktails.

Nobody in *The Cool World* has money for everything. One gang member's brother returns from fighting structural racism as a Freedom Rider, only to despair at its ravages in the form of poverty and crime. Duke's response is more instinctual. His inner

monologue indulges in youth-belying violent fantasies
in which he's king of the urban jungle, or gazes deep into
the abyss: "I see death everywhere." Clarke's trove of
vérité footage is distilled into a heightened, poetic truth.

Though her only two fiction features were shot in her native Manhattan, Clarke's trajectory was that of a runaway. Raised on Central Park West in an apartment with a half-dozen-odd servants, she turned to cinema and adapted the Living Theater's controversial play *The Connection* (1962), about jazz musicians and other junkies waiting for the man in a downtown loft. Though married with a daughter, she fell head over heels for Carl Lee, who played the heroin-pushing Godot. (Lee had a lifelong heroin habit himself; in her memoir *Life Itself!*, Clarke's sister Elaine Dundy writes that Clarke tried it as well, to better understand him.) Clarke and Lee adapted *The Cool World* from Warren Miller's novel, and Miller and Robert Rossen's play, and Lee is commandingly aloof as Duke's mentor Priest.

Clarke's films were difficult to see for many years (as *The Cool World* still is), ironically given that she cofounded the Film-Makers' Co-op along with Jonas Mekas and others. *The Cool World*, with its handheld street photography, is of a piece with the nonfiction impulse within the burgeoning American independent film movement, which achieved its purest form in the subsequent scrupulous filmography of *The Cool World* producer Frederick Wiseman. Clarke's interest in jazz and black life on the margins would continue in her only two features after *The Cool World*, both documentaries: *Portrait of Jason* (1967), edited down from an all-night interview with a hustler named Jason Holiday, and *Ornette: Made in America* (1984), about Ornette Coleman, the free-jazz saxophonist whose talent for improvisation perhaps equaled even Jason's.

What do people mean when they describe a film as "jazzy"? In the case of *The Cool World*, it partly means that the film runs tonal scales from biting open-air winter chill to hot-blooded youth, all set to a score composed and arranged by jazz pianist Mal Waldron for the trumpet deity Dizzy Gillespie's quintet. More generally it's an adjective that calls to mind Ted Croner's photos of late 40s New York City at night, or an Ornette Coleman solo: a bright, brassy clarity, smeared impressionistically into a high feeling, disharmonious notes rushing into your consciousness like the sensory overload of the city.

Clarke lent John Cassavetes the equipment he used to shoot *Shadows* (1959), his first film and, like Clarke's, one playing off the beats of postwar urban neorealism and showy, all-American jazz. Derived from acting exercises, the stop-start romance of *Shadows* interweaves narrative melodies on racial identity, sexual mores, and the struggle for artistic integrity. In the *Village Voice*, Mekas raved that an early version of

Shadows "proves that we can make our films now and by ourselves." Though Mekas disavowed Cassavetes's subsequent reshoots, which were more scripted and technically proficient (this is the version which is widely available today), the uncompromising For Us By Us cinema heralded by *Shadows* would be Cassavetes's legacy as the archetypal East Coast independent.

Cassavetes wrote *Gloria* to pry some cash loose from Hollywood, but was persuaded to direct it when his wife Gena Rowlands fell in love with the role of the title character, an aging moll who goes on the lam with a six-year-old Puerto Rican boy (John Adames), the sole survivor of a gangland hit. Though originating as a work-for-hire, *Gloria* is nevertheless recognizably a Cassavetes film: a study of a hard-loving maverick, embodied by his closest collaborator in a rich, sometimes cacophonous extended solo.

Seeking a sense of neighborhood life, Cassavetes shot *Gloria* far uptown, including in three different apartments in the same building on Riverside Drive at 158th Street. The film begins at the Concourse Plaza Hotel, at 161st Street and Grand Concourse, the "Boulevard of Dreams" of the Bronx's aspiring Jewish and Italian lower middle class in the first half of the 20th century; the building was city-owned and unoccupied, a former welfare hotel, by the time

Cassavetes showed up (he stopped his crew from cleaning up the graffiti on the walls). Yankee Stadium is just out the window, along with a snarl of freeways; the lives lived within these grand, forgotten prewar buildings seem an afterthought, suggesting something of the compromised history and teetering pride of Gloria herself.

With her whisky-soaked tough-broad voice, Rowlands conveys the experience that has honed her edge of irritability, and deepened her reserves of inner strength and loyalty. She hustles through the city—on and off busses, trains and cabs, in and out of lobbies, stairwells and elevators—with total gracelessness and absolute power. Her purse dangles from the shoulder of the same arm that fires a gun.

Cotton Comes to Harlem (Ossie Davis, 1970) / *New Jack City* (Mario Van Peebles, 1991)

Am I black enough for you?

So asks Deke O'Malley (Calvin Lockhart), of a Harlem crowd in batik-print caftans and church-lady poly-blend skirt suits and big hats, as khaki-uniformed militants look on. Fundraising for a back-to-Africa scheme, he has Marcus Garvey's mission—and James Brown's cape. After an assassination attempt, recalling Malcolm X's shooting in Washington Heights five years earlier, novelist Chester Himes's detectives Coffin Ed Johnson (Raymond St. Jacques) and Gravedigger Jones (Godfrey Cambridge) search, in poolrooms, soul food restaurants and tabernacles, for O'Malley and his money—both now missing, along with a bale of cotton that may hold the key to the mystery.

Everyone asks: what's a bale of cotton doing in Harlem? It's an echo of the antebellum world left behind in the Great Migration to the cities of the north, out of place in the neighborhood whose Renaissance authors inspired Himes, and, along with the Apollo Theater on 125th, made Harlem into black America's cultural capital. The film climaxes at the Apollo, on the sort of variety night that launched the careers of Ella Fitzgerald and James Brown. As Coffin Ed, Gravedigger and hope-hustler O'Malley scrap backstage, knocking over a Duke Ellington cutout and smashing props, they're literally fighting over—and around, and through—black culture.

Such would be the stakes of the cycle of African-American-targeted—and, sometimes, African-

American-made—blaxploitation films that followed *Cotton Comes to Harlem* and Melvin Van Peebles's *Sweet Sweetback's Baadasssss Song* (1971), hits in the old movie palaces of white-depleted cities. (Playing at the Loew's a few doors down from the Apollo in *Cotton* is Robert Downey Sr.'s anarchic comedy *Putney Swope* [1969], about a black executive who rebrands a Madison Avenue advertising firm as "Truth and Soul, Inc."—a parallel takeover.)

Director Ossie Davis's film reflects his politics: he had helped lead the festivities at the March on Washington, with his Harlem-raised wife and frequent Broadway co-star Ruby Dee. But heroin is fracturing *Cotton's* brightly lit Harlem village in Gordon Parks's *Shaft* (1971) and *Across 110th Street* (1972): the same neon lights and signs of 125th Street seem shot through a layer of winter grime. *Shaft* has a "Bumpy Jonas," *110th Street* a "Doc Johnson"— references to Bumpy Johnson, who ran numbers and dope in Harlem for the Genovese mafia family. In Gordon Parks Jr.'s *Super Fly* (1972), the pusherman antihero (Ron O'Neal) works outside "The Man's" network, like Harlem's real-life independent kingpin Frank Lucas; his white suit, pimped-out El Dorado, high-crown fedora and fur coat recall Lucas's flamboyant rival Nicky Barnes.

New Jack City was originally called *Nicky*, before producer Quincy Jones recruited journalist Barry Michael Cooper to rewrite an old script. Cooper had written "Kids Killing Kids: New Jack City Eats Its Young," a *Village Voice* cover story on Detroit's Chambers Brothers cartel, and written an early *Spin* feature on the crack epidemic, "the worst evil ever to hit Harlem," in the words of one of his interview subjects, a dealer to grandmas and dropout honor

students. Cooper's script for Mario Van Peebles's film turned smack into crack—and Nicky Barnes into Nino Brown.

As Nino, head of the Cash Money Brothers, Wesley Snipes gives a musical elocution to lines like "You gotta rob to get rich in the Reagan era." Though they feature funk soundtracks more up-to-the-minute than *Cotton*'s soul-gospel numbers, *Shaft*, *Across 110th Street* and even *Super Fly* followed the consciousness-raising Davis by emphasizing a desperate criminal underclass. By contrast, *New Jack City* updates the Depression-era gangsters played by East Side kid Jimmy Cagney. Cagney rose from the slums to the "top of the world," while Nino, to paraphrase Brooklyn crack dealer turned rap superstar Notorious B.I.G., drinks champagne when he's thirsty. Melvin's son Mario dresses his cast in Kangol berets and bucket hats; the Cash Money Brothers' bling glitters against vast primary-color double-breasted suits. They hold court behind a club where Public Enemy's Flava Flav and *Yo! MTV Raps* host Fab 5 Freddy emcee. Van Peebles does an Odessa Steps sequence at Grant's Tomb in Riverside Park, where Nino fires off approximately 9,000,000 rounds while dressed like one of the bellhops in Janet Jackson's Rhythm Nation.

The early 90s "urban" films boomlet coincided with the eclipse of hip-hop's Golden Age by gangsta rap, and the era's Harlem films feature West Coast rather than East Coast rappers: a DJ, in Ernest Dickerson's *Juice* (1992), and a schoolboy point guard, in the Cooper-penned *Above the Rim* (1994), see their ghetto-transcending gifts threatened by the thug life as represented by Tupac Shakur. In *New Jack City*, Nino's NYPD nemesis is Ice-T—a cult antihero offered up as an alternative to the social disintegration imbued by Snipes with more charisma than Deke O'Malley.

The CMB take over an apartment complex to become less a crack house than a full-on basehead Pentagon, where street soldiers with Uzis stand guard. Graham Court, on Adam Clayton Powell Boulevard between 116th and 117th Streets, is an eight-story palazzo built in 1901, with underground stables and mosaic floors to lure the fashionable crowd north of Central Park. By the 1960s, it was disintegrating under the weight of unpaid property taxes and neglected maintenance; here, the grand courtyard where a fountain once stood is as gray as zombie skin, with addicts fighting and tweaking, huddled over garbage fires—it's a synecdoche for the ravaging of black neighborhoods during the crack years.

Wild Style (Charlie Ahearn, 1983)

In *1990: The Bronx Warriors* (1982), shot not far from "Fort Apache," Enzo G. Castalleri served up spaghetti-a-la *Escape from New York* (1981) and *The Warriors*. A title card declares: "The Bronx is officially declared 'No Man's Land'. The authorities give up all attempts to restore law and order." At the time, amid white flight and the withdrawal of city services, with thousands displaced and neighborhoods uprooted by Robert Moses's slum clearance projects and the Cross-Bronx Expressway, absentee slumlords, squatters and arson had rendered entire Bronx

blocks burned or abandoned. Over the 1970s, the population of the Bronx decreased by more than a quarter of a million. *Wild Style* was shot in the fall of 1981, in a landscape that at times looks most of the way to postapocalyptic, where solitary flame-blackened tenements crumble amid weeds and piles of debris. But then, as Grandmaster Caz raps on the soundtrack:

> *South Bronx New York, that's where I dwell*
> *To a lot of people it's a living hell*
> *Full of frustration and poverty*
> *But wait, that's not how it looks to me*

Wild Style's genesis came when then-up-and-coming graffiti artist Fred "Fab 5 Freddy" Brathwaite brought Charlie Ahearn to a party in a concrete bandshell in a North Bronx park, where Ahearn was able to convince his future subjects he wasn't a cop. So that Ahearn could film DJs scratching live without having to clear samples, Freddy enlisted his friend Chris Stein, of Blondie, to put together instrumental tracks for the movie. By this time Freddy and other graffiti writers, like Lee Quiñones, Lady Pink and Zephyr, had started to show their work indoors at galleries like FUN on East 11th, whose co-owner Patti Astor would appear alongside them all in *Wild Style*.

Wild Style is just about a fiction film, with everyone playing versions of themselves; frequent performances cover the four elements of old-school hip-hop. There are rap battles in garage-like clubs with Busy Bee Starski, the Cold Crush Brothers and the Fantastic Freaks, and impromptu freestyling on metal-net basketball courts, stoops and backseats from the likes of Zulu Nation's Lisa Lee. Grandmaster Flash spins and scratches records in his kitchen. Breakdancers in Adidas roll out their floor. Quiñones breaks into train yards to throw up his pieces, then runs from the cops. The elevated subways of the Bronx provide a venue for competition between writers, and a rolling pubic art installation. We see the big bubble letters with bright highlights, and whole-car burners of cartoon characters and Campbell's Soup cans—Fab 5 Freddy's tribute to Andy Warhol.

The film came out ten years on from the rec-room parties where DJ Kool Herc first set up his turntables to loop the funkiest instrumental breaks from James Brown and the Incredible Bongo Band. By the time of *Wild Style*, Harlem's Sugar Hill Gang had had a hit with "Rapper's Delight" (some of which was likely lifted from Caz's unrecorded lyrics); Jean-Michel Basquiat, still known more for his ubiquitous SAMO© graffiti than for his paintings, had started hanging out with Warhol.

Patti Astor, who had previously acted in punk/No Wave films by Amos Poe and Eric Mitchell, plays a reporter taking an interest in what's no longer a strictly local scene. As the bottle-blonde Astor drives into the Bronx, the soundtrack cues up Blondie's "Pretty Baby". When Debbie Harry hosted the Valentine's Day, 1981 episode of *Saturday Night Live*, she also introduced "among the best street rappers in the country [...] my friends from the Bronx," the Funky 4 + 1 (including K.K. Rockwell and Lil' Rodney Cee, who appear in *Wild Style* as Double Trouble). As Astor drives back downtown, bringing Lee and Freddy to an art party in Manhattan, the song playing is, naturally, "Rapture".

At the party, guests include Glenn O'Brien, who edited Warhol's magazine *Interview*, and wrote the screenplay for the film *Downtown '81*, which starred Basquiat alongside Freddy, Harry, and too many other musicians and personalities to mention. At the "rock disco" the Mudd Club, Basquiat would DJ and play with his band Gray, "sort of punk jazz," Glenn O'Brien would write much later. He reflected: "Our scene, the corner of the world we lived in, was a funky musical comedy. Everybody made art, made movies and plays, and played in a band." In "Rapture," Debbie Harry began the first rap verse many Americans ever heard by spitting, "Fab 5 Freddy told me everybody's fly." *Wild Style* is of a rare moment when everybody— uptown and downtown, black and white, graffiti and galleries, hip-hop and New Wave—recognizes what's so fly about everybody else.

I Like It Like That (Darnell Martin, 1994)

Darnell Martin grew up on welfare in Morrisania, in the heavily Puerto Rican South Bronx. Her black father—a "disenchanted lawyer," Martin told the *New York Times*—wasn't around. Her white mother,

CHAPTER FIVE   147

a dancer and sometime commodities trader, wrangled Darnell scholarships to private schools in Manhattan and Connecticut, on and off; she'd find change in the couch to buy macaroni and cheese dinners for Darnell, her sister, and sometimes her sister's friends, when they were pregnant or hooked on heroin and had nowhere else to go.

When Martin made *I Like It Like That*, she was promoted as the first African-American woman to direct a studio film. To a sympathetic *Village Voice* interviewer, she called the marketing strategy "bullshit and horrible [because] it puts us in a subculture, subcinema." With mainstream outlets she was more diplomatic, shouting out to Leslie Harris's independently produced Brooklyn coming-of-age story *Just Another Girl on the I.R.T.* (1992). Martin was initially offered the budget for a seven-week shoot by New Line Cinema but held out for a year for a better offer: "I was about to be evicted," Martin told the *Times*. "But I thought, 'If I shot that film in seven weeks, it wouldn't be a good movie.'" After Columbia came through with two extra weeks, Martin kept fighting, to keep a number of scenes and her original ending. "Martin agrees that she can be loud," reported the *Times*, "but that it is usually in service to her work."

It was certainly loud when Martin shot *I Like It Like That* in her old neighborhood, on Findlay Avenue and 167th Street. Griffin Dunne, who appears in the film, told the *Times* about "200 radios playing from the windows, as if there was a big block party." In the film, neighbors holler at each other from fire escapes, and arguments spill out onto the street from the corner bodega, with its bright yellow, blue and red façade, and shelves shiny with cans of Goya beans.

In Lisette (Lauren Vélez) and Chino's (Jon Seda) apartment, with its greasy oven and chipping paint, the camera feels like an extra body in the room; long takes ratchet up the minute-to-minute intensity of life with three kids (whose faces are tattooed on Papi's arm). When Lisette locks herself in the bathroom for a minute's peace, her family screams at her through the door. The film has the volatile comic rhythm of catcall and comeback.

In the *Voice*, J. Hoberman compared *I Like It Like That* to *I Love Lucy*, and indeed the film concerns an NYC housewife becoming a frantic career girl more or less behind her cocksure, petulant husband's back. Chino all but declares that Lisette has some 'splainin' to do after she bluffs her way into a job with Dunne's yuppie music executive, who is grooming Lisette's favorite Latin pop heartthrobs for a crossover. (Lisette's mother-in-law is played by Rita Moreno, the only actually Puerto Rican star of *West Side Story* [1961] and a reminder of previous compromised representations of Nuyorican life.) The situations of this comedy arise from the challenges of keeping a family together when there's no money to take the subway to apply for a job: macho promiscuity, the push-pull of individual desire and stable traditional values, the fear of losing a child to drugs, overemotional parenting from adults who treat their children like adults because they're really children themselves. But though Darnell Martin, promoting *I Like It Like That*, would frequently describe her upbringing as "chaotic," there would always be a caveat: that doesn't mean it was unhappy.

The Royal Tenenbaums (Wes Anderson, 2001)

In *The Royal Tenenbaums* as much as in any of his films, Wes Anderson treats remembering as essentially a feat of imagination, and imagining as essentially a rite of remembrance. This family saga is a fairytale of New York dreamt by a Texan kid who grew up on the *New Yorker*, reading Lillian Ross's droll profiles and Joseph Mitchell's sepia yarns. When Anderson was in high school in the mid-80s, during the fourth and final decade of the pathologically discreet William Shawn's editorship and before the magazine began publishing photographs, a teenager reading the *New Yorker* would surely have felt less like an explorer of new frontiers than an archaeologist excavating a secret history. Each page, from Talk of the Town dispatches in first-person plural, to obscurely humorous "casuals," quippy cartoons, and book-length pieces on war or wheat, would have seemed a continuation of the witty, insular culture from which it sprang—and a reference back to it.

The young Wes Anderson was also partial to the quintessential *New Yorker* stories—precious, charming, fastidious—of J.D. Salinger, whose Glass children, in 50s works like *Franny and Zooey*, are like the Tenenbaums hungover from their prodigal childhoods, as stars of the prewar radio quiz *It's a Wise Child*. Tennis ace Richie Tenenbaum's center-court breakdown—filmed at the former home of the US Open in Forest Hills, Queens—mirrors Franny Glass's attack of catatonia, as Margot's depressive retreat to her bathtub mirrors Zooey's similar soak. The Tenenbaums' mocked-up Manhattan just keeps going and going, past neighborhoods you've never heard of, and further and further into the past, to places like the 375th Street Y, with its single-room occupancy tenants and rusty free weights on the roof. It's an alternate universe, familiar yet out of reach, like all the tattered books written by the Tenenbaums and dusty magazines featuring them on the cover. (The film is set in either a bygone time or a rarefied milieu in which print media affirms and reshapes the world.) The books may be the ultimate objects within Anderson's precise and handmade filmography: they're at once obsessively detailed and lovingly dog-eared, and you'll never get to read them. Each is a trace of something, just as every racetrack report, advertisement for a furrier, and theater listing in a back issue of the *New Yorker* finds its fanciful equivalent in every sports trophy, crayon drawing and taxidermied javelina hidden in a corner of the Tenenbaum house on "Archer Avenue."

For the Tenenbaum house, Anderson had been looking for a place "where you'd have a real strong sense of family history," he told the *New York Observer*. The house, at 144th Street and Convent Avenue in Hamilton Heights, appealed to Anderson for its fantastical aspects: he liked the heavy stone staircase and turret where all three of the Tenebaum children have their bedrooms, and the dead end down the street, shutting out the outside world.

The house was vacant, but had just been purchased by a finance type who, Anderson has said, essentially got it for free once fees for the month of prep and three weeks of shooting were factored in. The new owner was planning to renovate, but turn-of-the-century original features like the oak parquet floors and grand staircase were intact for the shoot—if a little bit creaky. (Anderson shot around newer features: the *Observer* reported that he "stopped filming once when he noticed a Medeco lock in a door that was intrusively new-looking; the director borrowed a pen and colored the lock all over to make it darker.") The roof, with its iron parapet, slate shingles and verdigris, had "this widow's-walk quality to it," said Anderson, whose production team slapped together a shed of weathered boards for Richie's falcon Mordecai—the urban rooftop pigeon coop, grown to the level of myth.

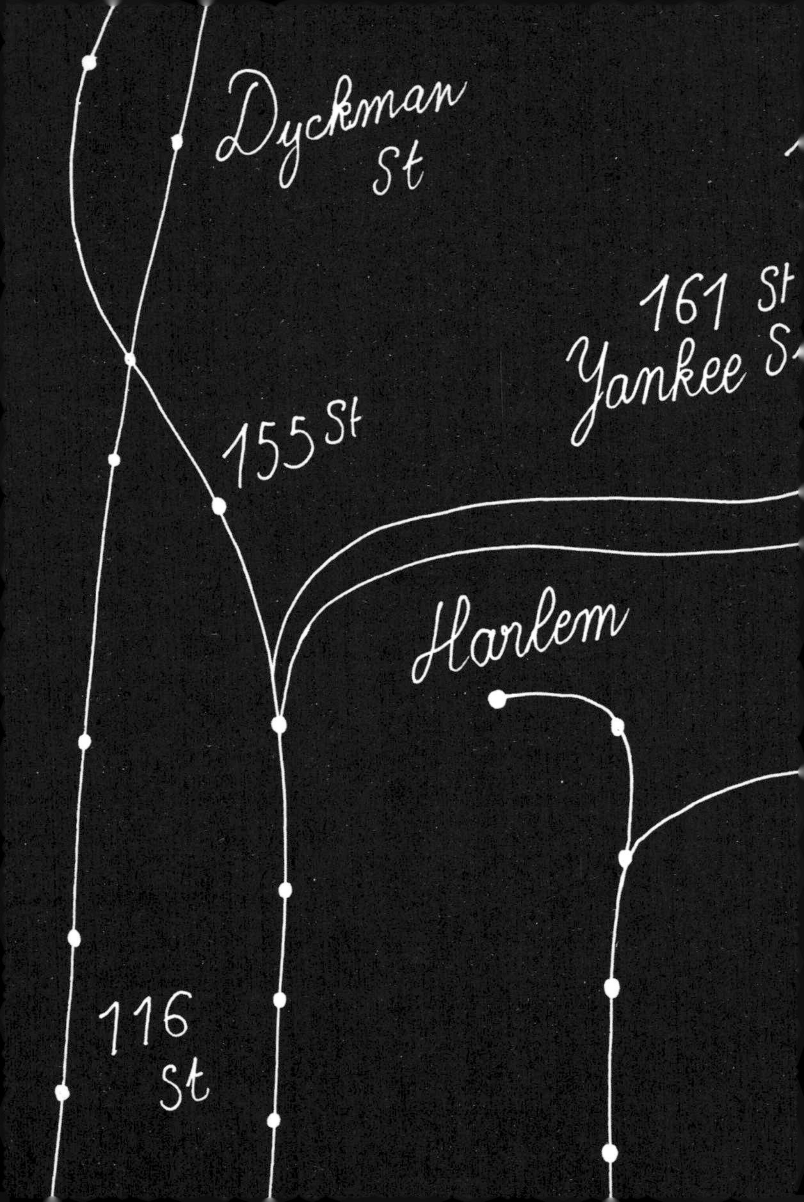
Dyckman St
161 St
Yankee St
155 St
Harlem
116 St

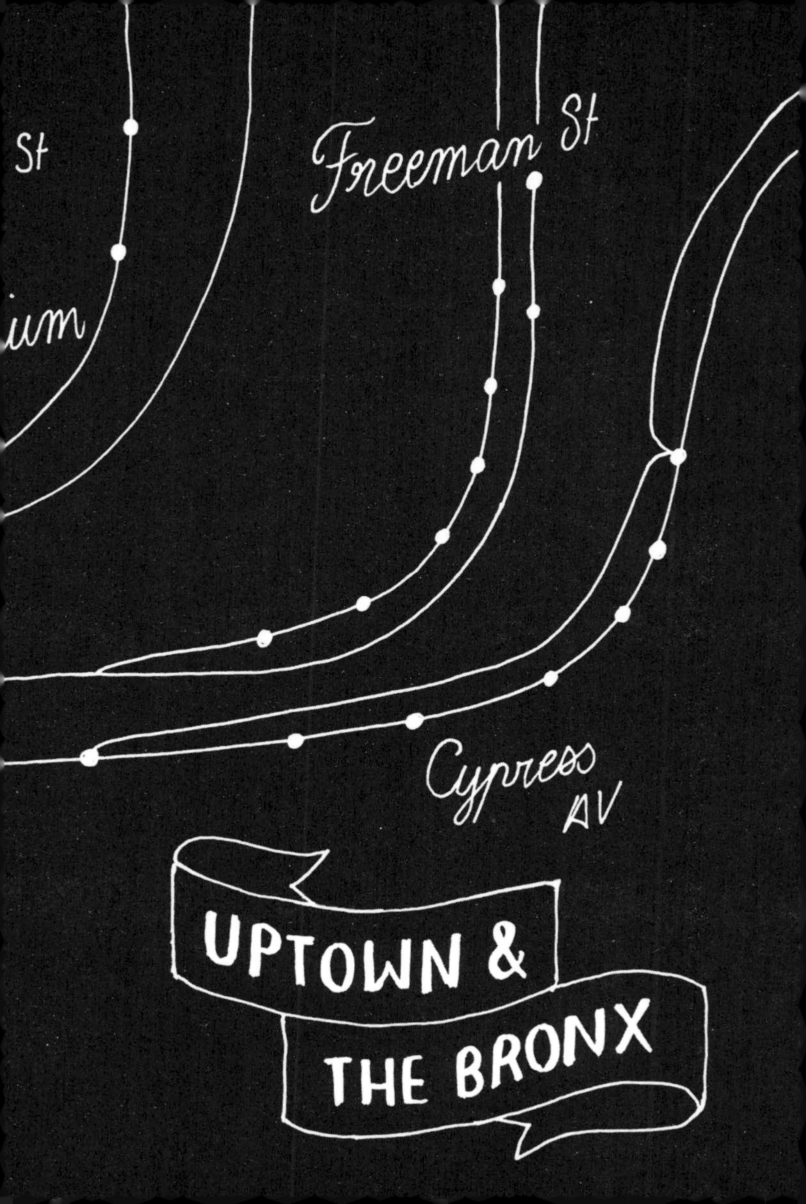

St

ium

Freeman St

Cypress
AV

UPTOWN &
THE BRONX

CHAPTER
SIX
BROOKLYN

Speedy (Ted Wilde, 1928) / *Little Fugitive* (Ray Ashley, Morris Engel and Ruth Orkin, 1953)

I n the decades before and after the turn of the 20th century, alongside the standardization of the weekend and other victories of the labor movement, the seaside resort of Coney Island evolved into "The People's Playground," a permanent carnival just a ride away on the new rail lines. At Coney Island,

the new urban consumer class could spend their hard-earned leisure time and pocket money sea-bathing, scarfing "hot dogs," gawking into funhouse mirrors, and riding the Shoot-the-Chutes and Witching Waves at Luna Park, illuminated at night with a quarter of a million electric light bulbs. The rise of amusement parks coincided with the rise of cinema, another mass entertainment which, in its infancy, thrilled the working classes with the wonder of modern technologies and views of exotic performers and faraway places.

Beginning in August 1927, slapstick star Harold Lloyd toured Gotham to film what would be his final silent comedy. *Speedy*'s four-week shoot stretched to twelve; Lloyd drew crowds to rival the summer of '27's biggest New York celebrity, Babe Ruth, who makes a cameo here, giving cinemagoers nationwide a glimpse of a star seen fleetingly in newsreels (and in a now-lost film, *Babe Comes Home* [1927], from *Speedy* director Ted Wilde). In one of *Speedy*'s several

extended chase sequences, Lloyd's baseball-obsessed cabbie delivers the Bambino to Yankee Stadium just in time to continue his chase for 60 home runs. The film turns the streets of New York into a dodgem-car ride, all whizz-bang metallic momentum—even though the primary plotline concerns Speedy's efforts to retain the city's last horse-drawn streetcar. (Though released after *The Jazz Singer*, this silent comedy has precious little Jazz Age flavor, aside from a stray bootlegging sight gag.)

On Coney Island, this was also the summer that the wooden Cyclone made its debut—it's still there, surely safer than it was in 1927, but surely feeling less so. Lloyd doesn't ride it, alas, in the scenes when Speedy and "his girl" head out to Coney for some time in the sun. Lloyd does close-quarters bits involving ice cream and balloons on a boardwalk as packed as a subway car, but subdues his straw-hatted cockiness as the camera takes in the same rides that Fatty Arbuckle and Buster Keaton had clowned around on in their two-reeler *Coney Island* (1917). The splashdown of the Shoot-the-Chutes log flume and the careening cars of the rippling Witching Waves oval provide the kineticism, until the camera becomes dizzy with superimpositions, dissolves, and other feats of cinema.

Rather than the avant-garde potential of a speedy futurist-utopian entertainment industry, *Little Fugitive* views Coney Island through the lens of poetic social realism. Morris Engel and Ruth Orkin— who married during the making of *Little Fugitive*, which they made with writer Raymond Abrashkin, credited as "Ray Ashley"—were members of the New York Photo League, whose members documented city life with the lyricism and crusading leftist spirit of much of the art, documentary and otherwise, to come out of the Great Depression.

By the time of *Little Fugitive*, Luna Park had burned down, pleasures-seekers were drawn away from the freak shows and waxworks to new entertainments, and developer Fred Trump was making the family fortune by overcharging the federal government to build segregated housing. Coney's eventual revival would be a nostalgic one, anchored by old institutions like Nathan's hot dog stand, and new ones like the Brooklyn Cyclones minor-league baseball team, as well as numberless filmmakers drawn to the symbolic nexus of neon, ocean, and playground on the edge of the city. In *Little Fugitive*, which Truffaut cited as a major influence on *The 400 Blows* for the youthful charge of its hidden-camera street photography, seven-year-old Joey (Richie

Andrusco, in his only film performance) runs away to Coney Island for the day. There, he loses himself in the throngs of bodies each on their square inch of beach, eats cotton candy and drinks Pepsi, throws the three baseballs at the milk bottles, and rides the carousel and pony. There's litter, seagulls—but in cataloging the raw impressions of a child, *Little Fugitive* distills Coney's sense of distraction and marvelment, as when the lights come up on the aptly named Wonder Wheel.

The Landlord (Hal Ashby, 1970) / *Desperate Characters* (Frank D. Gilroy, 1971)

In L.J. Davis's 1971 novel *A Meaningful Life*, a failed writer named Lowell Lake has a life-changing encounter with a real estate-section trend piece: "Creative young people were buying houses in the Brooklyn slums, integrating all-Negro blocks, and coming firmly to grips with poverty and municipal corruption," he reads. "It was the stuff of life." He buys an Italianate Clinton Hill mansion with good bones— and dried sewage in the basement, surly tenants in all the rooms, and the whole neighborhood filled with "old people proliferating in various degrees of madness and nudity, like some kind of ghastly, pale fungus." Davis himself had bought and renovated a townhouse in a Boerum Hill in 1965. Today brownstone Brooklyn is full of bistros and breeders, but Lowell Lake ends *A Meaningful Life* having spent all his reserves of sanity, fearful of his neighbors and of the contractors tearing the guts out of his house, and alienated from his home. The novel documents gentrification's original sin.

The Landlord likewise concerns a milky, insubstantial man who buys a Brooklyn property with plans to evict, renovate, and, at long last, make himself at home. Beau Bridges's 29-year-old Elgar still lives with his uptight WASP parents at their country manse, but he's one man ready to reverse the trend of white flight: "So, shit, I bought this house." The house is 51 Prospect Place, near 6th Avenue in Park Slope. The first time Elgar arrives to meet his new tenants, they chase him down the block as the neighborhood kids strip his hubcaps. When he tries to confront them over back rent, he's threatened with a shotgun.

The stairs are covered with moldy carpet and the wall paneling is chipped, but the building still retains original details, like stained-glass insets in interior lintels—enough for Elgar to dream on, anyway, despite the leaky pipes, rumored rats, and old toilet seats and limbless dolls strewn around the backyard.

But Elgar's house is already a home, as he discovers as he gets down at a rent party—though screenwriter Bill Gunn, director of the allegorical Brooklyn-and-upstate-shot black vampire movie *Ganja & Hess* (1973) and the experimental soap opera *Personal Problems* (1980), makes it clear that there are limits to the mixing of races. The racial and class politics of *The Landlord* are more forefronted than in the still-raging comment-section flame wars on New York real estate blogs, between those who parachute into a community thinking it's a fixer-upper and I Was Here Firsts telling "gentrifiers" to play in their own backyards, but the point of the film is the same: Elgar's house is already a home—it's just not his.

In *Desperate Characters*, an upper-middle-class white couple has the house, but there's nothing left. Adapted from a novel by Davis's neighbor Paula Fox, the film begins with a rooftop view looking north on Bond Street to where it terminates at the dome of the Dime Savings Bank, and pans east across bricked-up windows and backyards before zooming and dissolving into 396 Pacific Street, like a sneak preview of the neighborhood's future. Inside it looks like the *Landlord* house probably looks now, with Sophie (Shirley MacLaine) and Otto (Kenneth Mars) eating livers next to a two-story atrium with high bookshelves and a wheeled stepladder. Otto is complaining about the neighbors' music.

Fox made an early move towards establishing brownstone Brooklyn's reputation as a place for acute literary treatments of brooding bourgeoise. At dinner, Sophie's attention, like that of the likewise melancholy, childless wife in Hemingway's "Cat in the

Rain," is distracted by the stray at the back window. When the cat scratches Sophie's hand, the wound festers over a weekend of discontented encounters with ex-lovers and fading friends.

On Saturday night, Otto gets up from another loveless dinner and answers the door to a man who asks to use their phone—he smiles with his mouth as his eyes size up the house, and watch Otto and Sophie watch him. It's not a home invasion, but it's enough of an intrusion of the outside world into their Boerum Hill bubble that they take a Sunday drive to their country house. Otto, his lungs full of late-autumn air: "Who says you can't run away from your troubles?" But they arrive to a shattered sanctuary, and a local cop—played, with the tactless edge of his fiction, by L.J. Davis himself—delivers the message that they're not at home anywhere.

Saturday Night Fever (John Badham, 1977)

The definitive movie about disco, *Saturday Night Fever* sells a version that was largely the invention of a British flim-flammer dressing up his 60s memories in polyester.

When gonzo rock journalist Nik Cohn was new to the city, as he recalled in a 1997 retrospective essay, he initially sought out the soul, funk and Afrobeat rhythms then spreading outwards from "house parties," discotheques and members-only clubs filled with primarily gay, primarily black and Hispanic movers. But Cohn caught echoes of rock's eternal youthful escapist pulse emanating from the city's all-but-provincial white working class. At Bay Ridge's 2001 Odyssey, at 802 64th Street, a brawl broke out before Cohn got in the door, but not before he caught a glimpse of "a figure in flared crimson pants and a black body shirt, standing in the club doorway, directly under the neon light, and calmly watching the action. There was a certain style about him—an inner force, a hunger, and a sense of his own specialness. He looked, in short, like a star"—and reminded Cohn of awe-inspiring mods he'd known in Derry and Shepherd's Bush. This mythic figure inspired "Vincent," protagonist of Cohn's *New York Magazine* cover story "Tribal Rites of the New Saturday Night." Self-evidently a fiction of the Saturday-night-and-Sunday-morning school, its subjective cadences initially passed as an example of the New Journalism frequently published in the magazine—and seemed compelling enough to impresario Robert Stigwood, who had the Bee Gees and John Travolta both under contract.

So. There's Tony Manero, peacocking under the elevated B train on 86th Street (in Bensonhurst, but still) in flared pants and red platform-heel loafers to "Stayin' Alive," housing two slices from Lenny's Pizza at the same time, a big swinging dick in a small, still pond. Bay Ridge may as well be in another state from "the city"—even Tony's snobbish ballet-trained dance partner Stephanie (Karen Lynn Gorney), with her Manhattan office job, drops names with the gum-smack vowel sounds of an untamed Brooklyn accent.

At the Manero house on 79th Street, Tony's out-of-work construction worker father and sainted mother embody one side of the Catholic morality ingrained in Tony and his wide-collared, narrow-minded childhood friends. The other side comes out at night, when a woman is either "a nice girl or cunt," and the latter are the ones you make it with in the back seat. In the film, Tony and Joey and Double J and Bobby C. horse around on the cables of the Verrazano Bridge; in Cohn's story, they taunt the guard dogs chained across the street from the Odyssey: "They were drunk and it was late. They felt flat, somehow dissatisfied. And suddenly they threw themselves at the steel wires, yelling. [...] the dogs hurled forward again and again, in great surging waves, half maddened with frustration."

Odyssey 2001 is an unpromising space, surrounded by auto-body shops, except when Tony takes to the light-up floor (installed for the movie and kept until the club, by then a gay club called Spectrum, closed in 2005). He does the Latin Hustle, leads the whole club in the Bus Stop, or freestyles across the floor, pointing his finger from hip to sky. "[W]hen the other dancers fall back to watch him," Pauline Kael wrote of Travolta in the *New Yorker*, "it's because he's joyous to watch." Tony has an Al Pacino poster on his wall, and a little stardust of his own, as he wriggles into tight pink pants over black briefs, blow-dries his pompadour.

The film and soundtrack catapulted an urban scene into a national craze. White America ate it up—and then spat it out all over its "Disco Sucks" t-shirt. "It's a straight heterosexual film," Kael wrote, "but with a feeling for the sexiness of young boys who are bursting their britches with energy and desire—who want to *go*." The disco backlash reads as a renunciation of an "energy and desire" different than Cohn's reimagined rock-n-rollers letting off steam.

Tony and his friends are living romantic lives, but Tony's the only one who knows it. (Eliza Hittman's *Beach Rats* [2017] gives us a near-identical foursome, updated to oxy-tripping, vape-puffing Sheepshead Bay meatheads—and this time, the Tony Manero figure is gay.) At the movie's finale, an exhausted Tony finally takes the subway into Manhattan, probably staining his white suit as he leans into his seat beneath the rusty red spraypainted graffiti. On the Brooklyn-bound trains that time of night, in their own costumes, would have been the artistic kids on their way back from *The Rocky Horror Picture Show*, the new midnight-movie phenomenon in Greenwich Village, all of them looking just like Tony: so fabulous, so of their moment, but for now exposed, lonely, and in transition.

Do the Right Thing (Spike Lee, 1989)

His own best hypeman since at least the Nike ads he directed and co-starred in with Michael Jordan in the early 90s, Spike Lee has latterly taken on the role of Brooklyn block-party emcee, with annual all-day dance parties in memory of Michael Jackson and now Prince.

Lee's Brooklyn joints feel like block parties. The stoops and fenced-in asphalt front yards of Arlington Place, in *Crooklyn* (1994), or the Gowanus Houses projects, in *Clockers* (1995), become as familiar to you as they are to the neighbors who get together every year to close down the street to traffic, rent a bouncy castle, and lay out ribs and salads in single-use aluminum baking trays. In *Do the Right Thing*, the block is Stuyvesant Avenue between Lexington Ave and Quincy Street. Lee's crew hired locals to help replace the broken windows on the block's five uninhabited dwellings, and brought in muscle to shut down the block's crack houses (there are no drugs in the film, an absence many white interviewers pressed Lee on in 1989, to his anger). Today, on what's now known as Do the Right Thing Way, the new windows broken after the film crew left have been replaced again, and the paint is fresher than in the 1980s, though the "Bed Stuy Do or Die" mural graffiti'ed for the movie is long gone, as are the pizzeria and bodega sets built on vacant corner lots.

Do the Right Thing unfurls from one morning's wake-up call from DJ Mr. Señor Love Daddy (Samuel L. Jackson) to the next. Like in Sidney Lumet's *Dog Day Afternoon* (1975), dramatic tension rises with the mercury on the hottest day of the year; characters try to keep cool with shaved ices and an open fire hydrant before losing it altogether. Lee and cinematographer Ernest Dickerson burned a butane flame under the camera, for a shimmer that ignites the red-orange color palette and sportswear costumes. The film

opens on Rosie Perez dancing up a storm to Public
Enemy's "Fight the Power" (a song composed for
the film), and ends in a riot engulfing the entire
Brooklyn-in-a-block cast. There's Caribbeans
on the corner, a Nuyorican single mom, a white
brownstoner, a Korean grocer, and, of course, a
pizzeria, the life's work of Sal (Danny Aiello) and the
workplace of Mookie (played by Lee himself, a spry
smooth-talker like the Mars Blackmon character he
played in *She's Gotta Have It* [1986] and those Air
Jordans ads, a performance of blackness as much as
John Turturro as Sal's meathead son is performing
Italian-American). All the daily friction between city
tribes is eventually engulfed by the conflagration at
Sal's Pizzeria, when Buggin' Out (Giancarlo Esposito)
confronts Sal over his all-Paisan "Wall of Fame,"
and Radio Raheem (Bill Nunn) won't turn down
his ghettoblaster.

After the NYPD raises the temperature, the
crowd outside Sal's calls out the names of Michael
Stewart, beaten to death by the police who caught
him tagging the First Avenue L train station in 1983,
and Eleanor Bumpers, fatally shot by an officer who
brought a shotgun to an eviction in 1984. The film is
dedicated to the families of several black victims of
police violence, as well as of Michael Griffith, chased in

front of a car by a white mob in Howard Beach, Queens in a case that inflamed racial tensions in the winter of 1986-87.

Despite killing an unarmed civilian with a chokehold, *Do the Right Thing*'s Officers Long and Ponte are back on patrol in Lee's *Jungle Fever* (1991), in which they nearly shoot Wesley Snipes during a routine distress call. Months after *Jungle Fever*'s release, riots in Crown Heights would pit Brooklyn's African-Americans against Orthodox Jews over a child's death in a car accident and accusations of an official whitewash, in violence uglier and more fatal than the reprisal Mookie instigates here. For its depiction of state violence answered with black-on-white property crime, *Do the Right Thing* was, famously, called irresponsible or worse. In *New York Magazine*, David Denby declared that "if some audiences go wild, he's partly responsible."

Though it's the filmmaker himself who chucks a garbage can through Sal's window, Mookie's perspective is not the only one Lee offers. To argue over who in *Do the Right Thing* actually did "the right thing" is to miss the point of this often joyously polyphonic film. It's to value monologue over dialogue—to think about individuals, when the film is about a block.

While We're Young (Noah Baumbach, 2014)

Williamsburg was anointed a "New Bohemia" as early as 1992—rising rents had finally chased the artists all the way across the East River. A *New York Magazine* cover story followed them over, checking at places like the Ship's Mast, on Berry Avenue and North 5th Street. At that old seamen's bar and grill—a key location and de facto production office for Nick Gomez's *Laws of Gravity* (1992), a crime drama set among the neighborhood's lowlife—Irish and Polish truckers and plainclothes cops mingled with the drag-performer editor of the *Waterfront Week*, an alternative weekly photocopied in the back. Today's longtime Williamsburg residents are old enough to have seen its rezoned industrial waterfront metastasize in the late years of Michael Bloomberg's mayoralty into luxury hotels and condo developments like The Edge, with its "hardcore luxury" ad campaign appealing to buyers chasing the kind of cachet that's long since migrated down the L line to Bushwick. *While We're Young*'s music is by James Murphy, who, as the man behind LCD Soundsystem and a founder of DFA records, helped shepherd the area through its early-aughts PBR-and-trucker-hats guitar years

into its contemporary synthesized decadent phase. "The kids are coming up from behind," Murphy sang in "Losing My Edge," an aging hipster's lament, but the more acute anxiety is: what if they're coming somewhere else entirely?

At the start of *While We're Young*, Ben Stiller's Josh and Naomi Watts's Cornelia have the lives of Park Slope Babybjörn parents: he's a documentary filmmaker, she's a producer, and they live in a brownstone with airy kitchen extended by a bay window. Yet in the film's opening shots, they forget the story of the three little pigs when watching their friends' infant. (The kid's father, who shows off his sonogram tattoo, is played by Adam Horovitz—Ad-Rock, of the Beastie Boys.) Josh and Cornelia are alienated from their peers' social lives—she tags along to a parent-child singalong class that Baumbach edits like the *Psycho* shower scene, as if portending the death of any grown-up sensibility. It seems horrifyingly premature, given Josh's own stalled (or is it squandered?) potential.

An escape hatch presents himself in the form of Adam Driver's Jamie, resplendent with fedora and fixed-gear bicycle, who offers himself up as Josh's protégé. Jamie and his wife Darby (Amanda Seyfried) are 25—in a funny coincidence, Josh and Cornelia "were just 25" themselves—and live in "the Bush of Wick," in a loft with two kittens, salvaged furniture, a roommate and a chicken. They had a mariachi band and a slip-n-slide at their wedding. (Some of us are old enough to remember the "pool parties" that took over Williamsburg's McCarren Park Pool in the summers of 2006-8. Before the abandoned municipal pool was refilled for the actual children of North Brooklyn's working families, thousands of indie kids in cutoffs enjoyed concerts, food trucks, and—yes—a slip-n-slide.)

In Jamie and Darby's age bracket, everything is a discovery to be enthused over, even thrift-store Hard Rock Café t-shirts and Billy Ocean records. The couples' friendship unspools in montages as bright as a well-curated feed (unlike Baumbach's collaboration with his younger partner Greta Gerwig, *Frances Ha* [2012], which drifted into the cul-de-sacs of twentysomething confusion). The kids have no square hang-ups about hierarchies of high versus low culture—or, really, anything else. As Jamie fashions himself a nonfiction filmmaker, he's charismatically shameless about careerism, self-promotion, and finally documentary ethics. It sets him at odds with Josh, who's the right age to adhere, fussily, to the admonishments against "selling out" that would have held sway in the New Bohemia.

During Josh and Jamie's final showdown, at a Lincoln Center gala, the Gen X'er accuses the millennial of treating everywhere as his playground. It's a particularly New York take on the "you kids" rant. Surely at least some of the trust-fund kids who started going to Bushwick's artisanal pizza parlors during the Bloomberg years are now grumbling about sharing their tables with finance douchebags, and casting their eyes longingly towards that anarchist bookstore café a few more L stops into Ridgewood.

Nassau

Hoyt Schermerhorn

Propect Av

71 st

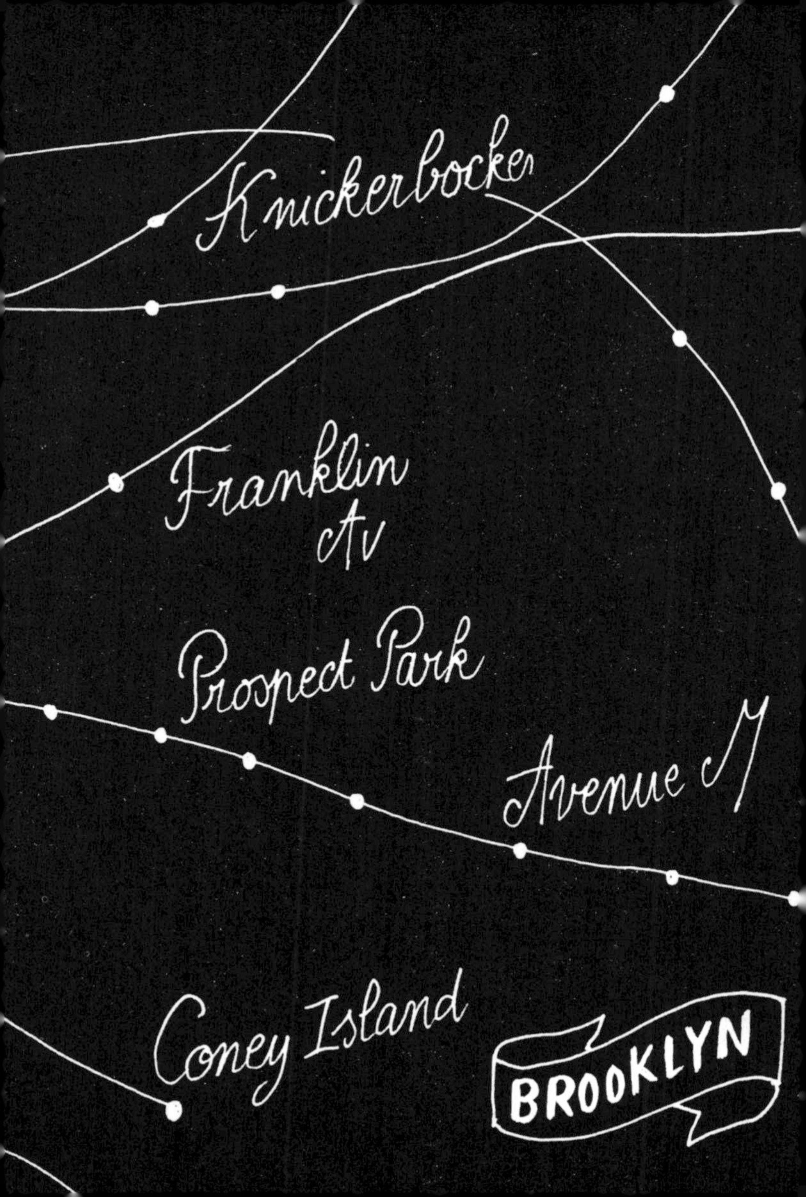
Knickerbocker
Franklin Av
Prospect Park
Avenue M
Coney Island
BROOKLYN

CHAPTER
SEVEN
QUEENS

The Naked City (Jules Dassin, 1948) / *The Wrong Man* (Alfred Hitchcock, 1956)

he Naked City was a landmark in the postwar American film industry's rediscovery of New York City. Inspired equally by the Italian neorealists and the true-crime photographer Weegee, the film became the template for a cycle of NYC noirs, like *The Window*, with a rawer feel than their Expressionist brethren. The film is heathered with street life, from ice wagons to organ grinders, and jittery with the energy of unpaid extras, as the murder of a department store model leads twinkly Irish policeman Barry Fitzgerald to a climax on a tower of the Williamsburg Bridge, by way of penthouse and tenement, switchboard and soda fountain, jeweler's shop, construction site, and a tidy policeman's townhouse and postage-stamp lawn in the metroland of Jackson Heights, Queens.

The film was the brainchild of producer Mark Hellinger, who before going West, was a celebrity newspaper columnist known for hardboiled, sentimental accounts of Broadway personalities. He provides the film's florid narration, in a mythmaking

I-love-this-dirty-town register. He concludes: "There are eight million stories in the naked city. This has been one of them."

Another: a 1953 *Life* magazine article about Manny Balestrero, who in the photo taken for the story stands on his doorstep in Jackson Heights, looking back over his shoulder into a spotlight as bright as an interrogation-room lamp. The article detailed how Manny had been called down from that doorstep and taken away by the police, accused of robberies committed by his doppelganger.

"I can see why it appealed to you," François Truffaut said to Hitchcock of the story, in their book-length interview: "a concrete, real-life illustration of your favorite theme—the man convicted of a crime committed by someone else, with all the circumstantial evidence working against him."

Hitchcock had shot in New York City previously and would again, integrating second-unit street pickups into *Saboteur* (1942) before its soundstage Statue of Liberty climax, and stealing shots of the United Nations building to go along with landmarks like the Plaza and Grand Central in *North by Northwest* (1959). *The Wrong Man*, his NYC noir, is a humbler affair, as Hitch avers in the introduction he gives in lieu of his usual cameo: "In the past, I have given you many kinds of suspense pictures. But this time, I would like you to see a different one. The difference lies in the fact that this is a true story, every word of it." According to an article in *American Cinematographer*, he told his frequent DP Robert Burks that he expected a "stark, colorless documentary treatment," to affirm the authenticity of the story (though Hitchcock did make changes, particularly weakening Manny's alibis).

Multiple *New York Times* articles reported on production, duly noting that Hitchcock was a "stickler" for accuracy while filming in the Queens courtrooms where Manny's trial was held, the Victor Moore Arcade on Roosevelt Avenue where the robberies took place, and Midtown hotspot the Stork Club, where Manny played bass. Yet, shooting in what is now a heavily Indian section of Jackson Heights, Hitchcock transcends true-crime gimmickry with scruffy, melancholy textures unlike anything else in his filmography: Henry Fonda, who plays Manny, reads the racing form at a late-night cafeteria on the way home from work, and picks up the milk from the steps of his stucco house as the IRT Flushing Avenue line rattles down the block.

In the film, Manny lives at 40–24 78th Street—you know because he repeats it so many times. Initially

it seems like the film is insisting on its realism, but it soon becomes clear that Manny is insisting on his sense of self. *The Wrong Man* is among Hitchcock's explicitly Catholic works—devout Manny, the son of immigrants, says his rosary in court, while his wife Rose (Vera Miles) suffers a nervous breakdown under the presumption of guilt. Hitchcock allowed to Truffaut that he was drawn to the point of view of the accused man, "ashamed" and ostracized from the world—a "subjective" approach contrasting with the procedural angle of most crime films of the era.

Many NYC noirs, following *Naked City*, gained their aura of authenticity through close cooperation with the police. Pre-"right to remain silent" authority in *The Wrong Man* is, by contrast, capricious—the NYPD frog-marches uncomprehending Manny to the liquor stores and groceries he's alleged to have robbed, parading him in front of witnesses and asking, this is the guy, right? All the while, the cops assure him that if he's innocent, he has nothing to fear. Salvation, the capture of Manny's double, comes as he prays for a "miracle"—but even once Manny's life is restored to him through divine intervention, Rose's paranoid conviction that the system is "fixed" becomes a surprisingly contemporary indictment.

Coming to America
(John Landis, 1988)

Where in New York can one find a woman with grace, elegance, taste and culture? A woman suitable for a king?

Saturday Night Live in the early 80s really was "The Eddie Murphy Show," as Murphy himself proclaimed on the episode he hosted while still a cast member. This was a time when *SNL* could catapult a streetwise, eager Bushwick kid to live-from-New York megastardom before his 22nd birthday on the strength of a well-delivered catchphrase. The characters and imitations in Murphy's early sketches and standup wed people-pleasing broadness to a frantic, edgy energy, all supported by ultra-precise fast-twitch muscle control and an agile vocal range.

That Murphy's range often extended into racial caricature feels, in *Coming to America*, appropriate to Queens's identity as the most ethnically diverse place on earth—it's an invigorating, brashly familiar take on the melting pot. In the film's barbershop scenes, Murphy, under Rick Baker's make-up, plays both the fast-talking middle-aged black man Clarence and the yiddishkeit Saul, whose respective gifts

of gab are matched only by their toleration of the other's bullshit.

Yet it must be said: when Murphy's African princeling Akeem arrives in Queens to live like common people and find his love match, the hovel he moves into—with vacant lots all up and down the block and a mural of dead Kennedys and Civil Rights leaders above the My-T Sharp barbershop—is actually in Brooklyn's South Side Williamsburg, on Hooper and South 5th Streets. Hand-to-mouth mid-80s Brooklyn must have seemed the natural setting for the winos in stairwells and homeless men at garbage fires which the film plays against Akeem's naïve out-of-towner grin.

Too, Akeem's Queens is not a foreign-language enclave, but the black bourgeoisie. Love interest Lisa McDowell lives with her father, a self-made fast-food millionaire—"See, they're McDonald's... I'm McDowell's"—in a Jamaica Estates mock Tudor outfitted with wet bar and La-Z-Boy. But *Coming to America* nevertheless hits on some home truths about the immigrant experience. The condescension with which the still upwardly mobile McDowell advises Akeem, his new employee, to pull himself up by his bootstraps is ironic, but also reminds us of the wild swings in fortune that go along with starting in a new place. It doesn't matter who you used to be: like the

Old Country yeshiva student-turned-Lower East Side sweatshop worker in Joan Micklin Silver's *Hester Street* (1976), to the Pakistani music star-turned-Midtown pushcart man in Ramin Bahrani's *Man Push Cart* (2005), Akeem must submit to low-wage labor.

And there's that face-straining grin Akeem wears whether he's mopping greasy floors, taking out the garbage, or expressing the good humor and gratitude he wishes to project—even though he lacks the words, even though he takes shit from the natives every day. It's the smile you see all the time in New York, on the faces of your deli guy, your Lyft driver, the breakfast-cart guy I used to buy my iced coffee from outside the York Street subway station who greeted every customer as "My friend!", never allowing themselves to appear anything but deserving and delighted to serve.

The Wedding Banquet (Ang Lee, 1993)

"He lived in an attic someplace in the East Village," a former professor of Ang Lee's told New York University's student newspaper in 2013. "And over his head, there was a sign. The first thing he saw when he woke up in the morning was 'Learn English.'"

It took Ang Lee a decade longer than his film-school classmate Spike to establish himself. His first feature, *Pushing Hands* (1992), was made with funds from the government of Lee's native Taiwan, as was its follow-up *The Wedding Banquet*, which became the nation's highest-ever grossing film, striking a chord with its treatment of familial bonds strained, but perhaps ultimately strengthened, across oceans and generations.

The Wedding Banquet's Wai-Tung (Winston Chao) has escaped his family's shadow, to a brownstone with his boyfriend Simon (Mitchell Lichtenstein), whose Keith Haring and Silence = Death t-shirts recall New York's very recent history of AIDS activism, and signal an out identity much more complete than Wai-Tung's. Wai-Tung is in real estate, and his tenants include his friend Wei-Wei (May Chin), a painter and cash-under-the-table waitress. To secure Wei-Wei's green card, and placate his parents—like Ang Lee's, Mainland Chinese who fled to Taiwan during the Chinese Civil War—Wai-Tung and Wei-Wei plan to marry. The charade involves redecorating with calligraphy scrolls, and Simon going back in the closet—but sneaking into the kitchen to secretly cook noodles for his boyfriend's parents, after years of practice. Chinese food here is

not white-carton takeout for the perpetually hurried, but a taste of home persisting in a city within the city.

When Wei-Tung goes to meet his parents at JFK airport, there is, among the deplaning passengers, and the throngs in the arrivals hall, not a single Caucasian face. It is a perfect bubble punctured only by Wai-Tung and Wei-Wei's double lives outside of it. Though purportedly set in Manhattan's Chinatown, where the predominant language is Cantonese, the film's centerpiece sequence, Wai-Tung and Wei-Wei's wedding banquet, was shot at the Sheraton LaGuardia East in downtown Flushing, Queens, where most Mandarin-speaking immigrants from Taiwan settled upon arrival in New York. Wai-Tung's conflicting impulses to assimilation and nostalgia find their fullest expression in a hotel ballroom done up in red and gold curtains, full of family friends and distant relatives from the city and beyond, and a few quizzical white colleagues. Traditions mingle: a baby jumps on the bed in the honeymoon suite—"to make a little boy like you"—and the bride tosses her bouquet. There's brown duck, red lobster, and the overfamiliar toasts and marathon drinking common to Eastern and Western weddings alike. One Mandarin-speaking guest exclaims, "This is a cross-cultural event—everything goes!", with a euphoria that's wired, liberated, and maybe even hopeful.

The Yards (James Gray, 2000)

James Gray was flagged immediately as a throwback—the *Village Voice*'s Amy Taubin called Gray's debut *Little Odessa* (1995) "closer to Visconti than Tarantino," and reported that *The Yards* would be, in Gray's own words, "my *Rocco and His Brothers*."

In *The Yards*, ex-con Leo (Mark Wahlberg), joins his flashy best friend Willie (Joaquin Phoenix), in the family subway-parts supply business, becoming ensnared in municipal corruption and the coverup of a death in the Sunnyside rail yards. Opening with a subway emerging from a tunnel, coursing along the veins of the city, the film is a bundle of blood ties and bonds of friendship. Thanks to the late great cinematographer Harris Savides, interiors are richly underlit and shot from a vignettish distance, recalling the Rembrandt-by-way-of- Gordon Willis look of *The Godfather* (1972). Sometimes there are blackouts—as befitting a film about politicized and flawed municipal services—and single gestures, or the contour of a face, lit by candlelight or headlamp, stand out from the darkness with an intense purity.

Gray's luxurious dramatic tapestries frequently weave unglamorous pictures of white-ethnic enclaves, from the vinyl-sided cop-land middle class of *We Own*

the Night (2007) to the sepia smog of the Jewish Lower East Side in *The Immigrant* (2013). Both *Little Odessa* and *Two Lovers* (2008) are Dostoyevskian dramas set in Russian-Jewish Brighton Beach, but while Gray's debut was a mafia story greenlit during the post-QT indie boom, *Two Lovers* stars Phoenix as a man on the cusp of inheriting the family dry-cleaning business. In the latter film's final shot, a stationary bike is visible, tucked behind a sofa.

For Leo, Gray wanted a "John Garfield" type— the real-life Dead End kid turned Method martyr —and found one in Wahlberg, an actor born to call his mother "Ma." Leo experiences the sentimental dilemmas and wild swings in fortune of a crime drama's tragic hero: Chasing a quick buck to provide for his sick Ma, he forgoes a union job as a machinist to join former partner-in-crime Willie as he greases the palms of the politicians and bureaucrats who award city contracts, sustaining Central Queens in a rusty echo of postwar blue-collar middle-class comfort despite slimming government and minority quotas. The film features a cameo from Keith Hernandez, a hero of the last Mets team to win the World Series, and the 1986 suicide of disgraced Queens Borough President Donald "The Boy Wonder" Manes looms heavy—not just in the backroom dealings but in the gray faces and thinning blow-dried hair of so many machine politicians.

Gray grew up in Flushing; his father, a partner in a firm that made electronic parts for the MTA, pled guilty to multiple counts of bribery in 1992. Gray told the *New Yorker*'s Tad Friend about his father's script notes: "He said, 'Don't have them using baseball bats to sabotage competitors' subway cars in the yards—that wouldn't look like equipment failure. Instead, we have them 'overvolt' the cars' electronics with a cattle prod.'"

Good Time (Josh and Benny Safdie, 2017)

The current generation of New York independent film inspires nostalgia without courting it. Resourceful, vérité-style filmmaking exposes the abrasive textures of city life—a palpable now-ness that can feel like a rearguard action in a place constantly overwriting old fads, old neighborhoods. The brothers Josh and Benny Safdie have earned comparisons to New Hollywood, but that's not to say their top-this appetite for out-of-the-way faces, places and vices is retro slumming—it's their birthright as city kids.

Good Time's cinematographer, Sean Price Williams, worked at Kim's Video, the legendary East Village chain of laundromats turned emporia of priceless cinema treasures burned onto glitchy DVD-Rs. His coworkers included writer-director Alex Ross Perry, whose burrowing Brooklyn dramas, like *Listen Up Philip* (2014), levitate above the everyday thanks in large part to Williams's intuitive, sun-mellow analogue photography. He shot the Safdies' junkie romance *Heaven Knows What* (2014) with long lenses, guerilla-style—an echo of Jerry Schatzberg's *The Panic in Needle Park* (1971), in which Al Pacino chased the dragon along the same wintry Upper West Side streets. Inspired by the experiences of star and first-time actor Arielle Holmes, and enacted by a cast of real-life addicts and crusties, *Heaven Knows What* feels like a nature documentary despite the neighborhood's wild places being far less visible today. In *Good Time*, Williams goes pore-close with a handheld camera, so that the 35mm film grain catches on the actors' stubble and blemishes. The movie is literally seamy.

Skin tones are jaundiced, and the light is the garish neon of rinky-dink arcades. It's as if all Queens is a queasy-making ride at Adventureland, the amusement park over the border in Long Island, where the characters break into the haunted house to retrieve a Sprite bottle full of acid. Hotfooting from Asian Flushing's New World mega-mall to unmopped fast-food bathroom to bail bondsman's storefront to no-money-down luxury apartment, the film follows the stupid, sordid odyssey of Connie Nikas, played by Robert Pattinson in a succession of puffy jackets and hoodies. After a bank robbery gone wrong, Connie endeavors to break out his accomplice: his mentally handicapped brother Nick.

Benny Safdie plays Nick—in interviews, the Safdies have said that, following the research that went into developing the character, they wouldn't have felt comfortable putting a disabled performer through the rigors of production, though the casting also continues the brothers' fascination with the kinds of people whose glances most New Yorkers avoid on the subway, training their eyes instead on years-old advertisements for dermatologists or personal-injury lawyers. (For posterity, *Good Time* features one of the last-ever late-night TV airings of the unforgettable Cellino & Barnes jingle—the law firm dissolved as the film bowed at Cannes.)

Native Manhattanites, the Safdies populate their films with nonprofessional actors: here, sick retirees, tired nurses, and a hyperobservant shrink with the beakish nose, deeply etched wrinkles and uncoiled-Slinky hair of a David Levine author caricature in the *New York Review of Books*. The drawling Buddy Duress, whom the Safdies met in the months they spent immersing themselves in *Heaven Knows What*'s milieu, and who gave interviews from the inmates' phones at Rikers Island as the film played the New York Film Festival, appears here as an ex-con whose life story plays like a single fucked-up shaggy dog story.

Good Time is structured like a farce, but the jokes

are surreally cruel, the perfectly timed pratfalls ending in ugly bruises or crushed hopes. The synthy score, by Oneohtrix Point Never, is a slick throb sometimes overwhelmed by dissonance, which seems an apt metaphor for *Good Time*'s take on the heist genre, and the city itself.

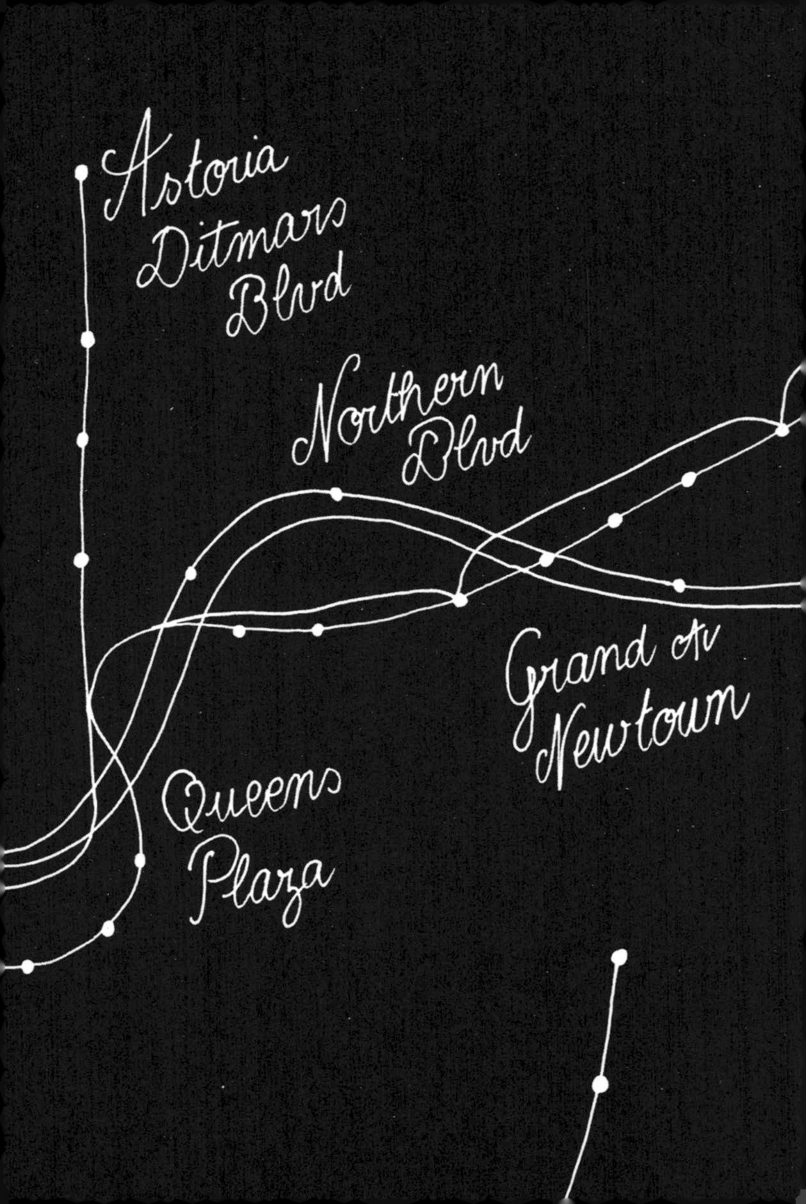
Astoria Ditmars Blvd
Northern Blvd
Grand Av Newtown
Queens Plaza

Flushing
Main St

169 St

Forest Hill
71 Av

Jamaica Center
Parsons/Archer

Kew
Gardens
Union Tpke

QUEENS

CONCLUSION

The Wiz (Sidney Lumet, 1978)

The last feature film shot at Astoria Studios before the Army took it over was *One Third of a Nation* (1939), an adaptation of a New Deal play starring Sylvia Sidney as a Lower East Side slum-dweller. Her gimpy kid brother was played by a teenaged Sidney Lumet, who would carry on the crusading social-realist spirit of leftist theater with his on-location New York films of the 60s and 70s. Lumet would earn a reputation for showcasing pungent performances and capturing a forgotten-man New York of wet-garbage gutters and grouty subway tiles, shoe-repair shops and fruit stands, next to which the media's Manhattan might as well have been Oz.

As so it is in *The Wiz*, Lumet's film of 1975's all-black *Wizard of Oz* stage musical. When Diana Ross's Dorothy et al finally arrive at the Emerald City, it's at the World Trade Center Plaza, where dancers and models promenade beneath the towers in furs and disco gowns by Halston, changing from green to red to gold to suit the fashion of the moment.

The Wiz is set in the New York of your wildest dreams. All the stories told in this book gain a hint of mystique from their proximity to images of genius or glamor or wit or struggle. *The Wiz* is pure icon-worship, set in a city comprised entirely of world-famous landmarks, using a combination of extravagantly art-directed locations and sets, built at the just-reopened Astoria Studios.

Dorothy and Toto land in Oz at the New York State Pavilion at the 1964 World's Fair grounds in Flushing, where Munchkins emerge from Day-glo graffiti painted on to hundreds of feet of walls built around that white-elephant relic of 60s futurism. After Michael Jackson's Scarecrow, with his Reese's Peanut Butter Cup nose, learns to walk on his boneless legs, the Tin Man (Nipsey Russell) is found beneath the real, creaky-looking Cyclone, and the Cowardly Lion (Ted Ross) among his stone brethren in front of a soundstage New York Public Library. They follow the Yellow Brick Road past matte paintings of the Chrysler Building and Brooklyn Bridge; the flying monkeys, here a motorcycle gang, chase Dorothy along the roof of Shea Stadium.

Yet throughout, Dorothy is, like the Warriors, trying to get home to Brooklyn. Though the script tells us that she's "never been south of 125th Street," she gives a Brooklyn address, 433 Prospect Place; in fact the building used for her house in exterior shots is further east into Crown Heights. Number 1097 is a four-story stone Renaissance Revival apartment building on a house-proud street in a black neighborhood, where

Dorothy's extended family gathers on Thanksgiving, to coo over the newest baby and play checkers and eat too much and sleep it off. It's there to which she finally clicks her high heels to return. There's no place like New York, but of all the fantastical things the city can be, it's also home.

SUGGESTIONS FOR FURTHER VIEWING

1. *Regeneration* (Raoul Walsh, 1915)

2. *East Side, West Side* (Allan Dwan, 1927)

3. *Force of Evil* (Abraham Polonsky, 1948)

4. *Killer's Kiss* (Stanley Kubrick, 1955)

5. *On the Bowery* (Lionel Rogosin, 1956)

6. *Sweet Smell of Success* (Alexander Mackendrick, 1957)

7. *Blast of Silence* (Allen Baron, 1961)

8. *Flaming Creatures* (Jack Smith, 1963)

9. *Barefoot in the Park* (Gene Saks, 1967)

10. *The Producers* (Mel Brooks, 1967)

11. *Klute* (Alan J. Pakula, 1971)

12. *Bijou* (Wakefield Poole, 1972)

13. *The Taking of Pelham One Two Three* (Joseph Sargent, 1974)

14. *Eyes of Laura Mars* (Irvin Kershner, 1978)

15. *Kramer vs. Kramer* (Robert Benton, 1979)

16. *Fame* (Alan Parker, 1980)

17. *Maniac* (William Lustig, 1980)

18. *Q: The Winged Serpent* (Larry Cohen, 1982)

19. *Born in Flames* (Lizzie Borden, 1983)

20. *Brother from Another Planet* (John Sayles, 1984)

21. *Moscow on the Hudson* (Paul Mazursky, 1984)

22. *Parting Glances* (Bill Sherwood, 1986)

23. *Moonstruck* (Norman Jewison, 1987)

24. *Full Moon in New York* (Stanley Kwan, 1989)

25. *Nadja* (Michael Almereyda, 1994)

26. *Smoke* (Wayne Wang, 1995)

27. *The Mirror Has Two Faces* (Barbra Streisand, 1996)

28. *Keane* (Lodge Kerrigan, 2004)

29. *The Devil Wears Prada* (David Frankel, 2006)

30. *Margaret* (Kenneth Lonergan, 2011)

31. *Pariah* (Dee Rees, 2011)

32. *Inside Llewyn Davis* (Joel and Ethan Coen, 2013)

33. *They Came Together* (David Wain, 2014)

34. *Person to Person* (Dustin Guy Defa, 2017)

35. *En el Séptimo Día* (Jim McKay, 2017)

William Collins
An imprint of HarperCollinsPublishers
1 London Bridge Street
London SE1 9GF

www.WilliamCollinsBooks.com
First published in Great Britain by William Collins in 2018

1

A catalogue record for this book is
available from the British Library.

ISBN 978-0-00-825664-7

Page 78: Extract from 'Greenwich Village' taken from Oh, Lady!! Lady!
(1917), lyrics by P.G. Wodehouse.
Page 143: Extract from 'South Bronx New York Subway Rap' by
Grandmaster Caz, from Wild Style (Animal Records, 1983)

Series editors: David Jenkins, Tom Killingbeck, Clive Wilson
Cover illustration by Christopher DeLorenzo
Interior illustrations by Laurène Boglio
Design and layout: Oliver Stafford, Laurène Boglio, Sophie Mo

Printed and bound by CPI Group (UK) Ltd, Croydon, CR0 4YY